FIRST FRUITS

First Fruits

14 SERMONS ON STEWARDSHIP

EDITED BY

DAVID MOSSER & BRIAN BAUKNIGHT

Abingdon Press
Nashville

FIRST FRUITS
14 SERMONS ON STEWARDSHIP

Copyright © 2003 by Abingdon Press

This book is printed on recycled, acid-free paper.

Library of Congress Cataloging-in-Publication Data

First fruits : 14 sermons on stewardship / David Mosser and Brian Bauknight, editors.
     p. cm.
Includes bibliographical references.
   ISBN 0-687-02512-5 (pbk. : alk. paper)
   1. Christian giving—Sermons. 2. United Methodist Church (U.S.)—Sermons. 3. Christian giving—United Methodist Church (U.S.)—Sermons. 4. Sermons, American. 5. Christian giving—Sermons—History and criticism. 6. Christian giving—United Methodist Church (U.S.)—Sermons—History and criticism. I. Mosser, David, 1952- II. Bauknight, Brian Kelley, 1939-
   BV772.F475 2004
   248'.6—dc21

2003002555

05 06 07 08 09 10 11 12—10 9 8 7 6 5 4 3 2
MANUFACTURED IN THE UNITED STATES OF AMERICA

Contents

PREFACE

Hilarity and mirth often mask our deepest anxieties. For example, about ten years ago I led a group of moderately young church leaders through their first *bona fide* "Fall Stewardship Campaign." Naturally, what most churches call the fall stewardship campaign is generally a code word for "budget raising." To this end, our congregation's veteran leaders determined that our church's next generation needed a direct and hands-on experience in financial leadership. Thus, our young leaders learned personally of what raising a nearly one million-dollar budget consisted.

To inaugurate this crash course in faith finance for beginners, I led a Bible study and stewardship reflection. Afterward, the youngish committee chose a theme and delegated individual responsibility for this essential undertaking. We all sensed a certain tension in the atmosphere. Perhaps most of those eleven people gathered understood that their church's ministry was at stake. They knew that churches with financial problems experience more sustained anxiety and pressure than churches without monetary troubles. Each person present that night felt a deep responsibility, for they all loved their church.

I selected the story of Ananias and Sapphira for our meeting's meditation (Acts 5:1-11). This story is so chilling that most lectionaries tend to pass over this text. In fact, most of those present that evening were unfamiliar with the story. After I concluded my remarks, the group discussed Ananias and Sapphira at length. Suggestions for our church stewardship campaign theme came pouring out. The most appealing theme, and the one that best captured the group's imagination, was a succinct slogan. One young man said, "I know! Let's use the theme: 'Give or Die.' " We laughed about how on target this theme was. The group decided the "Give or Die" slogan would be easy for our congregation to remember since it was short and to the point. This crass slogan also conveyed plainly the message of Acts 5. Sensibly, we all knew that this theme would have been inappropriate, even offensive, for a church-wide stewardship campaign. Ironically, however, we all also realized a deep truth—hilarity and mirth often mask our deepest anxieties. Our excessive laughter that evening symbolized the modern mainline church's anxiety about speaking to the issue of financial stewardship.

Without question, a stewardship campaign focuses on the management of a congregation's fiscal resources. Realistically, however, stewardship in its broadest definition of "managing the whole household" is a year-round endeavor for church leaders. It sounds a constant refrain in the life of the church because it is one of the most tangible practices of discipleship. To be a disciple is to practice stewardship in all its manifold expressions. Teasching, listening, visiting, praying, leading, organizing, and giving are each forms of stewardship of which there are hundreds, and possibly more, diverse expressions. Pastors, as leaders, need to help people come to terms with each member's God-given gift to offer something to Christ's church through stewardship. As one of my preacher colleagues fondly pronounces, "Giving leadership is leadership giving." In other words, if pastors expect those who follow us to respond, then we must ourselves do what we ask of others. The best leaders have always understood this principle.

When Brian Bauknight and I decided to pursue the collecting, editing, and writing of this compilation of sermons (with the excellent help of Ronda Wellman in putting this manuscript in its final form), we based our decision on several obvious and practical realities. Each autumn for nearly twenty-five years, each of us has experienced the challenge and frustration of raising a church's budget for the subsequent year. When we were relatively young pastors emerging from seminary, what we knew about spreadsheets, giving patterns, and deficit spending was minimal at best. Yet our congregations looked to us, as their pastors, for leadership, even in areas in which we possessed little experience. Although both of us were longtime church members prior to entering seminary, we had had little opportunity to sit in on the day-to-day decisions about church finance.

In light of these concerns, we enlisted the help of some of the best preachers we knew to assist pastors in their reflections on stewardship in the context of preaching. Preaching is where we homilists articulate practical theology in both appropriate and understandable ways to congregations. For several decades, many old-line and mainline churches have balked at opportunities to teach this vital aspect of discipleship to its people. If we are to regain a toehold in the authentic teaching of discipleship, then the pulpit is one good place to begin.

This book includes some well-known North American preachers and a variety of prominent voices from among those accomplished in the art of preaching. Many contributors are pulpit ministers, while others have had wider responsibilities in the church and, in one instance, the synagogue. While many of the contributors happen to be United Methodist, and several sermons are offered from preachers of other Christian traditions, not all are strictly Christian. Rabbi Wenig's sermon addresses a stewardship of hope offered to her New York temple congregation. The sermon approaches offered here are eclectic, but all of them primarily focus on the theme of stewardship.

One distinctive feature of this book is a brief analysis at the end of each sermon about what made that sermon "work." Anyone who has ever preached will remember a sermon that was received poorly in the congregation while later, in the narthex, someone expressed thanks for the message we had just considered a "clinker." Preachers live with the words that Jesus spoke to Nicodemus: "The wind blows where it chooses, and you hear the sound of it, but you do not know where it comes from or where it goes" (John 3:8). We never know how a congregation may hear our sermons and, consequently, rely on the Holy Spirit to buoy our meager efforts. At the same time, it is important for us preachers to offer our best homiletic endeavors. The analysis of these sermons attempts to underscore those sermonic features we believe are most helpful.

Is stewardship preaching the single most important topic that preachers address in sermons? Clearly, the answer is "No." However, for most believers, stewardship is the most hands-on realization of discipleship. Through stewardship, we participate in something much greater than the narrow world we create. Through stewardship, God offers us a way to become co-creators in the great enterprise of life. To be able to articulate stewardship from the pulpit is to offer a congregation an invitation to discipleship in a clearly tangible and concrete way. After all, stewardship does not simply happen once a year. Rather, stewardship is a lifelong process of understanding, growth, and decision.

We hope and pray that, in these sermons, you may find fuel to burn your imaginations. Then perhaps you may help your congregation catch a new vision for faithful giving. Every preacher I know needs fresh insights into the vital theme of stewardship. We hope you can find some new and creative ideas within the pages of this book.

David Neil Mosser

Introduction:
VISION-DRIVEN GIVING

The church needs a new vision for giving because old strategies no longer seem to work. Clergy and lay people cry for help. They regularly express the desire for a whole new way of looking at stewardship and giving in the local congregation.

Doing ministry today costs more than ever. A preacher of an earlier generation tells of a globe he bought for his grandchildren as a Christmas gift. Since they had asked him for this gift, he gladly obliged. However, when they unwrapped the globe on Christmas morning, Grandfather sensed disappointment in their eyes.

"Is something wrong?" he asked.

"Well, Grandpa," came the reply, "we sort of hoped for one with a light inside it."

Grandfather dutifully went out and traded the one globe for a newer unit with a built-in light. A few weeks later, someone asked him what he had learned from the Christmas incident. He replied, "I learned it costs a lot more to light the world today."

Indeed it does. Basic costs of doing ministry continue to esca-late. Full-time, part-time, and stipend staff are needed to equip members for ministry and mission. Communication with new generations of believers and seekers requires computers and tech-nical enhancements for sanctuaries. Health and pension costs for clergy and lay staff rise regularly, just as they do in virtually every secular business in today's economy. Truly, it does cost more to light the world today.

Preaching and teaching stewardship provides a fascinating challenge—the subject becomes difficult because people often do not wish to hear about it. Congregations want better funding for their church's ministry, but they do not want the preacher to address the matter from the pulpit. Routinely, a church's person-nel or pulpit committee imposes restrictions upon the clergy. "We don't want to tell you what to preach, but don't talk about money," they tell the pastor. "That's one subject we don't like to discuss around here."

On occasion, the subject of finance becomes a difficult topic because members of the clergy often have their own problems with personal financial decisions. Speaking about giving when one feels trapped in a financial straightjacket is no easy matter. We hope this book will bring light and energy to the subject of money in the context of Christian discipleship.

I enjoy preaching about money. My goal in preaching about stewardship is to never be confrontational, but always invita-tional. I try to help all believers (including myself) to grow from wherever they are to the next step where God wants them to be. To this end, I offer ten suggestions for effective, faithful, biblical, and theologically appropriate stewardship preaching.

1. BE BOLD

Boldness is the only way to address money and giving. We apologize far too much for our stewardship sermons. Here are two examples that serve to negate the biblical principle of stewardship:

"Today is stewardship Sunday. Sorry about that!"

"Next week is our annual stewardship drive. I'm telling you that now in case you want to plan for elective surgery or a root canal!"

A preacher can be proactive, assertive, and courageous without being harsh or judgmental. Some interesting facts undergird this principle. The Bible contains about five hundred verses on the subject of prayer and a similar number on the subject of faith. But it holds more than two thousand verses on the subject of money and possessions! We have approximately thirty-eight of Jesus' parables recorded in the New Testament. Of these, there are sixteen about money and possessions—more than any other single subject. Some might argue that Jesus spoke more about the kingdom of God than about money. However, several of Jesus' kingdom parables are about the subject of money and possessions. In addition, one could easily make the point that the proper use of money is a major part of "kingdom living."

Can you imagine Jesus saying to the so-called Rich Young Ruler, "I don't want to offend you, sir, but you really ought to recognize your misplaced priorities?" Or can you imagine Jesus concluding the parable of the man with many barns by saying, "I hope this is not intimidating to any of you, but you probably need to know that a person's life does not consist of the abundance of his possessions?" Finally, can you imagine Jesus watering down his statement about earthly treasures? "I don't want to be misunderstood here, but you might want to consider the fact that earthly things tend to corrode and rot way. Keep that in mind."

Boldness is the only way to go. We do not run over people; we remain sensitive to legitimate differences in life situations and resources. But we speak boldly in the name and authority of Jesus on this issue.

2. BE ENCOURAGING AND UPBEAT

We are bearers of the encouraging word. We never scold or chastise; those who may need a dose of Christian discipline are usually absent anyway. We will not shame people into giving. We will not induce guilt by reminding folks that our denomination has among the lowest per capita giving in the nation!

We offer hope and encouragement at every turn. The record is clear—generous givers are typically more spiritually vigorous and happier than those who are not generous. In addition, this fact has nothing to do with the size of the gift. Rather, it has to do with our level of generosity with whatever we happen to have.

We can remind people of a joyous truth: God's work done in God's way will never lack for God's supply. I have often observed that not one church in a hundred has any notion of its power.

I preached my first sermon as part of a college deputation team near Valley Forge, Pennsylvania. I took as my text for that morning these words: "Always be ready to make your defense to anyone who demands from you an accounting for the hope that is in you" (1 Peter 3:15). I've long forgotten the point of the sermon, but the text empowers me to this day. When we speak of giving, we speak in hope.

Sometimes, hope seems elusive, especially during times of church financial campaigns. Nonetheless, we hold fast to our hope. A few years ago, our church entered a financial campaign for the construction of a Christian Life Center and other ministry enhancements in the amount of $3.3 million. Everything in the campaign pointed toward total success. We were certain we would raise $2.4 million in the first phase—perhaps even the total amount. Many in the congregation knew the statistically promised results. They arrived for worship on "Celebration Sunday" with great enthusiasm.

I had announced the sermon title earlier in the week for this special day: "Reasons for Rejoicing." However, we had all hoped for better results. We ended that campaign with pledges amounting to $1.6 million which grew, over ensuing weeks, to about $1.8 million. A second campaign raised about $1.2 million. At the time of our 50th anniversary as a church we owed about $1 million because of accrued interest. I made some quick adjustments in my sermon that day, but held to the spirit of the title. I said we had reasons for rejoicing because:

• We experienced great fun and celebration in the process.
• We raised more money than at any previous time in the history of the church.
• We had enough money to do what God wanted us to do!

I tried to provide three solid reasons for rejoicing. Because of the blessing I had helped our people articulate in their hearts, we left worship that day on a high and positive note.

3. ALWAYS PUT GIVING IN THE CONTEXT OF DISCIPLESHIP

The mission of the church is to build, form, and sustain disciples. The aim of stewardship development is not to finance the church's annual operating budget but to change lives. Giving is part of discipleship. Giving is part of our spiritual formation. When God breaks in upon a sufficiently prepared people, a new generosity emerges—one that is outgoing, joyous, spontaneous, and free.

Preachers serve their congregants best when they help believers keep the focus. Giving is a discipleship issue. Use the terms of discipleship each time you preach, write, or teach about giving in the Christian life. Bake sales, bazaars, and beef dinners build great fellowship in the church, but fund-raisers are not discipleship. Money gimmicks may make people smile or even laugh, but gimmicks are not discipleship.

A certain church experienced difficulty raising enough money for their new building. A candy factory in town had a faulty run of lollipops one week, and could not sell the product on the open market. The church approached the owner of the factory and asked permission to sell this particular supply of candy as a fund-raiser for their new building. The owner agreed. They raised the money, but word around town was that defective suckers built that church. Good preaching always makes discipleship, not fund-raising, the central issue in church finances.

For many years we used the "barometer" motif in my church. Each year, we erected the barometer at the back of the sanctuary to show progress toward a stated dollar goal. We never reached the stated goal. As we moved toward an exclusive emphasis on discipleship in recent years, the barometer came down. The goal today is not a dollar figure; rather, the goal is growth in discipleship. Today, in my church, no new budget is written until that year's "financial faith promises" are in hand.

4. SHARE YOUR OWN EXPERIENCE

Tell your own stories about giving. Share the struggles, the joys, and revelations. I often relate my first awareness of giving as a child. I began delivering newspapers when I was ten years old and collected payment from customers every Thursday evening.

When I came home after my first night of collections, my father was waiting for me in my room with a box of church offering envelopes in his hand. "How much did you earn?" he asked. I was unsure, so he helped me count the money. We carefully allocated the amount that went to the route manager and the amount that I could keep. My share was $3.50. "OK," he counseled. "You put 35 cents into your church offering envelope as your 'tithe' to God. The rest is yours to keep or spend as you determine." I have never forgotten that evening. Nor have I regretted his guidance. I also recall listening to my parents discussing their giving at the evening dinner table. My wife and I have since made important decisions about discipleship giving during our own journey. We have experienced times of doubt that later became moments of great promise and celebration.

I often say that I have discovered I can live better on 90 percent of my income than I can on 100 percent. Today we live better on about 85 percent of our income. With gratitude to God, my wife and I have been able to increase our household annual budget giving to just over 15 percent of our current income. At that level, we are convinced we are more blessed than ever! In addition, we periodically tithe our accumulated savings for special campaigns. God is good all the time.

I eagerly tell of my struggles and the joys as I preach and teach. I find that such stories resonate with more experiences in people's lives than I can possibly know. How do I decide what to give? How do we make decisions about "extra" giving? What has been the procedure in our home and marriage when we feel we are "tapped out" or "tithed out"?

5. MODEL GOOD "GROWTH GIVING"

We pastors must model good giving, but more importantly, model good "growth giving" to the church. Don't think your people don't know about your giving—they do! I remember a frank discussion with a finance chairperson from a larger church. He said, "Brian, our pastor doesn't give to this church!" I agreed to talk to the pastor.

The pastor and I met later that day. The pastor acknowledged that he had some very unusual ways of "giving" to the church—none of which found their way into the general ministry budget. As we talked, he finally recognized a great truth. "I have been obeying the spirit of giving, but cheating the church," he said. Before the campaign ended, he and his wife had pledged 13 percent of their income to the ensuing year's church budget.

Do you believe in giving to the church? Do you believe in tithing? Do you believe in growing toward tithing? Can you model a growing edge? Consider doing so in faithful, non-boastful ways. You and the lay leadership in your church set the pace for growth giving in your gathered faith community.

6. PREACH TITHING

I have tithed all my life. In my parents' home, we tithed on every bit of money that came in. I love to tithe. I find that tithing gives me an opportunity for significant giving and substantive discipleship. I also find, although I cannot rationally explain it, that tithing gives me greater control over the rest of my resources.

Too often, many persons under fifty years of age know little about tithing. The word and the biblical concept itself are foreign. What people do know about tithing seems cold and legalistic to them.

Try not to get caught up in the details of tithing. Net or gross? Adjusted growth? Salary or benefits? Cash income or investments? Instead, talk about how you make those decisions, and also encourage people to make their own choices in this regard. Invite them to move toward a tithe of *something*! Work to raise five to ten new tithers every year in your congregation and make it part of your annual ministry goal.

7. PREACH THE "GIFT OF GIVING"

For some believers, tithing is an insufficient objective. Many people have the spiritual gift of giving as part of their call from God. The Bible lists approximately twenty-five spiritual gifts given to believers. Among the gifts are pastoral care, teaching, administration, leadership, and hospitality. Giving is but one of our God-given spiritual gifts. Announce the "gift of giving" in your preaching. Recognize that the gift is present in your place of worship on any given day.

I initially learned about the gift of giving from a lay member of my previous congregation who invited me to lunch one day. As we shared a meal, he told me that he and his wife wanted to make a contribution to the "seed fund" for a major building program that our church envisioned. He handed me a check for $25,000. I was dumbfounded. No one had ever given a gift of that magnitude in any church where I had served. He then explained. "Brian," he said, "we are doing this for two reasons. First, God has richly blessed our lives and we want to share those blessings with our church. Second, I want to use this opportunity to challenge you to seek others like us to make significant gifts to the church and the work of God's kingdom."

Several years later at a new church appointment, I asked for a large gift toward a new pipe organ for our church. The man asked me an unexpected question: "How much do you want?" I was both surprised and unprepared. My mind raced for an answer. Finally, I offered, "What about $18,000?" I quickly added, "Over three years, of course."

He smiled and said, "Fine, we'll do it. But you need to know that you didn't ask me for enough!" Here was a Christian couple with the clear and demonstrable gift of giving.

Another man said to me at a breakfast meeting one morning, "For some reason, God has given me the ability to make a lot of money. I need you to help me make sure I use that gift wisely."

A few years ago, my financial secretary came to me with some information about a gift to our capital campaign. She informed me of the gift of a single woman who spent most of her life in United Methodist mission work and was a person of limited financial resources. My secretary said, "Few people will ever know how much this woman pledged to this campaign. But you need to know that it was a generous and substantial gift for a woman of her means."

The point is this: lay people have taught me an exceedingly important truth about the promise of scripture and the power of spiritual gifts. I now try to open up two or three new "gifts of giving" in my church each year. I refer to this gift as often as I can. I give the gift of giving as much visibility as possible.

8. BE CREATIVE WITH TITLES AND TEXTS

Let your mind and heart discover fresh titles and texts that capture the imagination and challenge the spirit. Listen for words and phrases that easily form into titles and images.

Sermon on the Amount

Right on the Money

A Farewell to Alms

Fit to be Tithed

Blessed be the Tithe that Binds

The Sounds of Substance

(Some of these titles, and the message to go with them, appear in my *Right on the Money* from Discipleship Resources).

Have fun with titles and use imaginative texts. As I write this, I am working on a message for our stewardship Sunday with the title "All the Best" using the text from Numbers 18:29. "Out of all the gifts to you, you shall set apart every offering due to the Lord; the best of all of them is the part to be consecrated."

Some years ago we held a stewardship effort that placed signs around the church for several weeks. The signs simply said "TIYC SDAW." No explanation was given. People thought the signs had something to do with stewardship but could not discern the meaning of the letters. Finally, someone correctly determined that the first four letters stood for "This Is Your Church." Guessing games began regarding the other four letters. One suggestion: "So Donate A Wad;" another, "Sit Down And Weep." The actual solution was fairly simple: "Seven Days A Week."

One year, we engaged in a capital campaign to liquidate our mortgage. After much discussion, the planning team decided on the theme, "To Free the Future." Just before the meeting adjourned, someone offered another suggestion. "Why don't we just call it 'Dump the Debt?'" His comment initiated a whole new flow of ideas. The end result was captivating. A local contractor placed dump trucks in the "up" position at each major entrance to the building. Each truck had a sign greeting worshippers that read "Dump the Debt!" In addition, someone purchased small toy dump trucks, had special cards made for them, and mailed them to every member of the congregation.

Have fun with texts, titles, and themes. Stretch your imagination. Make stewardship a time to look forward to with each new season.

9. USE HUMOR

Christian people love to laugh at themselves. Money and the church often have humorous applications and I enjoy collecting some wonderful stories. In fact, I have preached many stories multiple times over the past ten years.

Comedian Jack Benny had a reputation as an inflexible tightwad. One day, in a skit on his radio show, a would-be robber stopped him on the street, poked a gun into his ribs, and said, "Your money or your life." After a long pause, and a few more jabs with the gun, Benny quipped, "I'm thinking, I'm thinking." The preacher of a small Methodist church in England used the theme from that skit for his sermon on stewardship Sunday one year. His title: "Your Money or Your Life." That morning, the choir's anthem was the familiar "Take my Life."

Humor enriches good stewardship preaching.

10. PREACH FOR THE LONG HAUL

Set some long-term goals for your stewardship development. Let your goal be to build giving disciples. Most people will grow best in gradual steps—incremental growth feels more realistic to most realistic people. Remember to teach and preach this principle in each new season: *Grow from wherever you are now to the next step where God wants you to be.*

In all probability, major overnight advances in giving will be few. Most people move upward by gradual steps. Our call as preaching pastors is to cultivate new givers and new "conversions" (toward tithing and the gift of giving) each year. Our hope and prayer is that this book will assist you to that end. As you read, internally dialogue with, and reflect upon the resources and sermons in this book, may you receive an energy surge in giving, in ministry, and in your own discipleship.

Brian K. Bauknight

CHAPTER ONE

"STEWARDSHIP: THIS SIDE OF THE ESCHATOLOGICAL DIVIDE"

Ronald J. Allen

Ronald Allen describes the context for this particular sermon:

As a guest preacher on stewardship Sunday, I preached this sermon to a central Indiana congregation. My full-time ministry is teaching at a theological seminary. Congregations occasionally invite me as a guest preacher. The invitation usually comes when the local pastor is on vacation, when the congregation needs a substitute preacher, or when stewardship Sunday rolls around. Local pastors and fund-raising committees seem to enjoy having a guest deliver the sermon on the day that churches receive pledges. My impression is that this desire stems from two roots. First of all, local leadership thinks a guest preacher gives pledge Sunday a special quality. They perhaps believe a visiting preacher provides such an occasion greater importance and, hence, may increase the size of the pledges. The other reason, I would guess, is that a fair number of preachers feel a certain discomfort when preaching about money from the pulpit. Having a guest relieves them of this task while still getting the subject into the air.

This county seat congregation had a morning worship attendance of about 100 and is over 100 years old. Like many congregations in the long-established denominations, the membership is weighted towards persons over age 55, with just a few younger people. The congregation's membership has declined steadily for years. I have known the pastor for over a decade. The congregation does not have any deep institutional problems.

I selected this text and focus because I had been teaching exegesis of the book of Romans at Christian Theological Seminary. The study of Romans intrigued me. Especially noteworthy was the relationship between the offering of the Pauline churches for the congregation in Jerusalem and the eschatological motif of the wealth of the gentiles (nations) flowing towards Jerusalem. I checked with the local pastor and discovered that the church had not heard a sermon on this theme in recent years. The pastor thought that the congregation might find it a refreshing way to deliberate their financial giving.

"Stewardship: This Side of the Eschatological Divide"

Romans 15:22-29

I wish I had asked the church secretary to include a map of the ancient Mediterranean world in our bulletins this morning. We would then notice something odd. Picture these three places. Jerusalem is at the east edge of the map. Corinth is about 800 miles across the Mediterranean west. Rome is about 600 miles further west than Corinth.

Now Paul writes the letter to the Romans from Corinth. Paul wants to visit the congregation at Rome, a mere 600 miles from Corinth. In fact, the word "wants" does not do justice to Paul's feeling. "I desire, as I have for many years, to come to see you when I go to Spain." The term desire (Greek: *epipothia*) is exceptionally strong. It refers to a deep and persistent longing. Paul yearns to visit Rome because it will mean that the apostle is on the last leg of his journey to Spain. Spain is the goal of his missionary career because, symbolically, it represents the end of the earth. Paul wants to go to Spain, and stop along the way at Rome. But here is the odd part. Paul says, "I am going to Jerusalem in a ministry to the saints; for Macedonia and Achaia have been pleased to share their resources with the poor among the saints at Jerusalem." It is really odd that Paul is in Corinth, merely 600 miles from Rome, when he suggests, "but first, I must go 800 miles back to Jerusalem, then retrace those 800 miles and add an additional 600 miles to Rome." He could scoot the 600 miles from Corinth to Rome, but, instead, he travels a total of 2,400 miles.

My spouse and I live in Indianapolis. One summer we took a 25th wedding anniversary trip to Alaska. You may know that Alaska is north of Indianapolis. The great price on our airline ticket took us from Indianapolis all the way south to Dallas before we started north for Alaska. Despite the great price on the ticket, I was quite annoyed that we had to spend seven hours in extra travel going south before we could go north. Paul did not have the advantage of jet speed. He traveled in a ship powered only by the wind. Why go 2,400 miles when he could go only 600 miles? We are talking about a difference not just of hours or days or weeks but of months. Yet Paul delays one of the major goals of his life, reaching Spain, so that he can return to Jerusalem. Why this detour?

"At present, however, I am going to Jerusalem in a ministry to the saints; for Macedonia and Achaia have been pleased to share their resources with the poor among the saints at Jerusalem. They were pleased to do this, and indeed they owe it to them; for if the

Gentiles have come to share in their spiritual blessings, they ought also to be of service to them in material things." The "saints" are the congregation in Jerusalem. The "ministry to the saints" is an offering that Paul has collected in congregations in Macedonia and Achaia regions around Corinth.

If we were hearing Paul's words with the ears of first century Jewish persons, we would hear Paul's decision on two simultaneous levels. At one level, concern for the poor is fundamental to Jewish identity and to covenantal community. To be in covenant is, by definition, to accept the care of the poor as a part of the community's identity and responsibility. To allow poor people to remain poor is an injustice, a violation of community identity, and will bring about the eventual collapse of the community.

Our family lives on the edge of an impoverished area. Every time we drive downtown, we pass through blocks and blocks of poverty. These people dwell in houses with paint peeling, no grass in the yards, no cooling in the summer and no heat in the winter—some without water. People stand on the street corners, their faces as vacant as the empty lots where houses have burned. Each time I make this drive, a biblical perspective hangs like a weight on my heart. How long can our nation allow such poverty before we collapse? The congregation in Jerusalem is poor. The congregations in Macedonia and Achaia would remember words like those of Deuteronomy, "I [God] therefore command you, [the community], 'Open your hand to the poor and needy neighbor in your land' " (Deuteronomy 15:11). Paul returns to Jerusalem to carry the offerings that express the covenantal community's care for the poor.

On another level, first century Jewish people would feel another resonance in Paul's action. Isaiah writes in a time when the Jewish people were poor, discouraged, and oppressed by gentiles. Yet this prophet looks forward to a day when "You [Israel] shall see and be radiant; your heart shall thrill and rejoice, because the abundance of the sea shall be brought to you, the wealth of the nations shall come to you . . . they [the Gentiles] shall bring gold and frankincense, and shall proclaim the praise of the Lord" (Isaiah 60:5-6).

Isaiah anticipates a time when gentiles will acknowledge the sovereignty of the God of Israel. They will turn away from the things that characterize gentile life: idolatry, injustice, covetousness, selfishness, antipathy and even violence towards the Jewish people. The gentiles will turn to the living God and covenantal community. They will bring offerings to the God of Israel in Jerusalem. These offerings will contribute to the material wellbeing of the Jewish community. A great reunion will take place between the Jewish and gentile peoples. All will be blessed. By Paul's time, many Jewish people believed that the great day that Isaiah anticipated would take place at the end of history. The technical theological name for that occurrence is the "eschaton," a word that means "last things."

The adjective is the long, strange word in the title of this sermon: "eschatological." It refers to qualities of the last day, the day when all things will be as God intends them to be. Do you remember Paul's mission? He is apostle to the gentiles (see Romans 1:1-5). Through Paul's ministry the great reunion between Jewish and gentile peoples is taking place. Through Jesus Christ gentiles acknowledge the sovereignty of the one, true, living God of Israel and are being welcomed into community with God and with the Jewish people. Paul delays his trip to Spain because he believes that the offering for the church in Jerusalem is a part of the wealth of the nations flowing into Jerusalem. Yes, the collection in Macedonia and Achaia provides relief for the poor. Yes, the offering fulfills covenantal identity. But even more than this, the offering is a sign that the eschatological world is unfolding. The offering represents the merging of the gentiles with the people of Israel into the one great community of God. From this standpoint, financial stewardship is not just supporting the institutional church by helping meet the mortgage payments and keeping the gas bill up to date and buying curriculum and paying the pastor. Financial stewardship is an eschatological witness.

You and I are gentiles. Through Jesus Christ we have come to know, love, and serve the God of Israel. When you and I make a contribution to the church, we acknowledge that the wealth of the nations belongs to the one, true, living God. We confess that we believe that God is even now at work eschatologically; that is, we believe that God is at work remaking the world. God is aiming toward abundance for all and poverty for none. God seeks a world in which people of different races and cultures live together in justice and love. God is leading to a world in which violence gives way to mutual support and peace. By making a pledge to the church, we say that we are not willing to settle for the world as it is with its racial discrimination, its economic exploitation, its idols and injustices. Rather, we pledge that we join God in working for the coming of God's new world in which love and justice characterize all things.

Now, unfortunately, I have to interrupt this beatific vision with some facts. The actual practice of the church does not always fulfill Paul's attractive vision. I have known church treasurers who were constitutionally unable to write a check for world outreach. Frankly, in my denomination much of the money that we collect under the rubric of "outreach" only pays for services for congregations and pastors. We have long heard that Sunday is the most racially segregated hour of the week. Our churches struggle with issues of race on many levels. Recently several African American students spoke with me and requested that the seminary call an African American as a visiting professor. These students wanted this visiting professor to offer a course in preaching in the African American tradition. A European American and an African American teach our introduction to preaching course. Our preaching courses all contain materials by African Americans in the core readings. These courses all focus on African American preachers. Class discussions intentionally take up themes that are important in the African American tradition.

Yet, this approach did not satisfy these students. I asked them to help me understand the reason for their request. They replied, "We appreciate what the seminary is doing. We feel included. But you may not know what it's like always to be the minority, sometimes to be the only one in a class. We need our own setting." Our seminary, like other seminaries, has been working at racial love and justice for a long time. But even with the best intentions, we often find ourselves in situations of brokenness and pain that are characteristic of the old world. Hence, stewards must continually ask a practical question of the church: "Are we using the money that we receive in optimum ways to help facilitate the eschatological world? Or might we be using that money to rein-force the old world with its ways that need to be replaced?"

As long as we live this side of the eschatological divide, in a world in which sin is a penetrating power, we can expect the church's life to be less than the life of the eschaton. I hasten to add that negative attitudes and behaviors in the church and the world do not obviate the eschatological vision. Furthermore, the letter to the Romans helps us understand that giving to the church, by definition, commits us to the eschatological world. If our witness falters, then God finds others who join the move-ment towards the eschaton. We can see the eschatological hope taking shape around us, and even participate in it, from time to time. For example, one of the most prominent dimensions of the eschatological world for Paul is the reunion between Jewish and gentile peoples.

Unfortunately, not long after Paul's ministry this relationship took a wrong turn. Since shortly after the time of Paul, many Christians viewed Judaism with a disdain that has sometimes turned violent. At first, the synagogue and the church were in conflict over a variety of things concerning the ritual law and the Messiah. This theological conflict eventually escalated into anti-Judaism, which in turn led to anti-Semitism, and finally mani-fested itself in the Holocaust. Gratefully, in our time many Christians are repenting of this aspect of our history and are seek-ing reconciliation with Jewish people. A rabbi teaches regularly at our seminary. A handful of divinity schools have Jewish schol-ars on faculty. Many Christian and Jewish congregations meet regularly for worship, study, and dialogue. One of my colleagues speaks not of the Christian mission to Judaism but of the mission that Jewish and Christian congregations share. Few religions have had such fractious relationships as Judaism and Christianity. But when two millennia of suspicion, hatred, and violence can begin to give way to mutual respect and common mission, we can have the confidence that we can similarly transform other antagonisms.

Giving money does not solve such situations. But financial stewardship is one way that we say "Yes" to God's vision of the new world and our willingness to join God in helping the new world come to life. I began with an oddity, and I close with one. I have been speaking as if we sign onto the new world through making a pledge. And that's true. But the other side of the coin is true too. Eschatological vision often changes us and makes it possible for us to become better stewards than we ever imagined in our old world patterns of thought. The eschaton empowers us. A few years ago a visitor from Lesotho came to our congregation with the story of a need in that land in southern Africa. The people in his part of Lesotho were living in hunger and poverty with few educational resources and very few pastors for many congregations. The congregations had begun to offer classes in better use of the land to provide food, instruction for jobs, and instruction in reading and mathematics. But they had a big problem: just one pastor for every twenty congregations, and the pastors had to travel on foot from one distant congregation to another. The people needed the pastors not only to lift their spirits, but also to help them provide the instruction in agriculture and reading. Could our congregation help them buy a horse, an ideal mode of transportation in their part of the country bereft of roads and sources for gasoline? B. J., a fifth grade friend, sits down the pew from us. He catches a vision of what the horse can mean for people in Lesotho. For a week, instead of eating lunch, he sets aside his lunch money for the horse. Now remember, he is only in the fifth grade and has no lunch for a week. When he brings his money forward the next week, his face is joy itself.

How long has it been since you have felt that kind of eschatological joy? So, when you sit prayerfully with your pledge card, Paul invites you to see your pledge as more than a financial commitment to the church, more even than an act of care for the poor. Paul invites you to recognize that your pledge is a vote in favor of God's new world, and a sign of your promise to work with

God in its coming. How much is that world worth to you to help light with the gospel?

An Analysis of Ronald Allen's "Stewardship: This Side of the Eschatological Divide"

Ron Allen gives this congregation a solid sermon in a difficult preaching circumstance. He is neither the pastor nor given a simple preaching task. Rather, he preaches on the "Bermuda Triangle" of preaching topics—stewardship! Yet, Allen preaches well, judging from the sermon text. I want to suggest ways in which Allen's sermon "works."

One beneficial thing Allen's sermon does is to help listeners understand the context from which Paul writes to the Romans. Allen plainly explains why Paul goes "to Jerusalem in a ministry to the saints" (Romans 15:25). Thus, Allen delicately reminds his listeners that stewardship is not a recent church occurrence. Rather, stewardship is a response of long-standing and tradition-laden discipleship.

Allen also helps listeners connect with the biblical principle of stewardship. In addition, Allen links stewardship to the eschatological doctrine of the end times. Allen reminds all believers—Jews and gentiles—that we belong to God's eschatological community. This is a faith community that cares for and shares with others. Consequently, Allen anchors the theological principle of stewardship in a biblical understanding of God's working through us on "this side of the eschatological divide."

Allen's use of illustrations (a map, a poor neighborhood, contemporary race relations, and a fifth grade student) encourages the congregation to envision the deeper theological principles to which Allen alludes. Allen, as a preacher, paints a picture with his words for the listener's imagination. They not only hear the sermon, they also "see" it!

One of the chief outcomes that preachers can glean from Allen's sermon is that, if carefully developed, even something as daunting as a stewardship sermon can help people relate to the Bible in new and creative ways. Not only this, but Allen clarifies that one of the Bible's fundamental theological doctrines—stewardship—is also a doctrine that disciples observe in conventional daily life.

CHAPTER TWO

"BIRTHRIGHT ON THE MARK DOWN TABLE"

René Rodgers Jensen

René Jensen describes the context for this particular sermon:

I've always been fascinated by the story of the quarreling brothers Jacob and Esau. One day as I was reading the passage in which Esau sells his birthright, it suddenly struck me that this was a great scripture for a stewardship sermon. After all, we each struggle with the temptation toward immediate gratification and the issue of what is truly valuable over the long term.

I preached this sermon as a part of the annual stewardship campaign in our congregation. Because we mostly preach stewardship sermons in that context and because we usually discuss stewardship connected with money, most lay people (and perhaps most pastors!) tend to think of stewardship primarily, if not exclusively, in terms of a financial commitment.

This sermon's goal was both to acknowledge that connection, and nudge the listeners to think of the larger implications of their financial commitment, and, indeed, how they use their financial resources. Our congregation is a typical middle-class church with many members who live comfortable lives and for whom Christian financial stewardship is not a high priority. In this sermon I wanted them to begin to think about the ways in which all of us are tempted to settle for the immediate gratification of our material wants and settle for a transitory satisfaction of a fleeting desire. We hold far too cheaply our identity as children of God and our obligations as members of Christ's body.

"Birthright on the Mark Down Table"

Genesis 25:29-34

Old man Isaac had a right nice spread of land. Rolling acres of tilled farmland and green pastures, with a stately house perched proudly on the highest hill. The biggest farm in the county, and one day it would all go to his oldest boy, Esau.

Isaac and his wife, Rebekah, had two boys. They were twins, but those boys were as different as night and day. The oldest by only a few minutes was Esau, but most folks called him Red, on account of his bright red hair and his broad, perpetually sunburned face. Red was his daddy's favorite. He was a boy any daddy could be proud of because he was always hunting and fishing, bringing home the choicest bits of game for his daddy to eat. Perhaps not the smartest boy in the world, truth be told, but a good boy nonetheless. Everybody liked Red; he was always laughing and joking, ready for good time. He was captain of the football team, big and brawny and strong as an ox—and about as smart. Still . . . a good boy.

Now Jacob, Red's brother, he was the smart one. He was smooth and pale from staying indoors. Jake was his mama's favorite. Some said he was tied to her apron strings. Jake was always thinking, although he rarely said too much. But you could see his deep-set dark eyes take in everything, trying to figure out how he could turn it to his own advantage. Jake was slicker than a greased pig on the Fourth of July. Folks tended to come away from an encounter with Jake with an uneasy feeling that they should count the fillings in their teeth to make sure they were all still there.

Red and Jake were as different as two brothers could be, so maybe it was no surprise that they fought all the time. They had fought from the time they lay side by side in their mother's womb. They fought about everything. They fought over what was the best fishing hole in the county and where you could find the best wild mushrooms; over who would take Mary Sue Barnes to the prom and the best way to skin a deer. But at the root of their constant fighting was the festering knowledge that one day the prosperous farm, with its rich rolling fields and fat cattle and proud white farmhouse, would all belong to Red. All his life, Jake had lusted for that farm, while Red, the center of his daddy's life, took his inheritance for granted.

One day Red had been out hunting. Although he had been out all day, he'd scarcely got off a good shot, much less hit anything. By the time Red got home, he was tired and dirty and cold and hungry enough to eat an ox. When he came stomping in the kitchen, cussing and muttering, his nose met the most wonderful smells. Jake had been cooking.

Now maybe he was a sissy, the way some folks said, but Jake was a great cook. He'd learned to cook from his mama, Rebekah, but now he could teach her a thing or two about how to use a stove. He could make biscuits so light they plumb floated out of the pan and his cakes were like a little taste of heaven. His chocolate cake had won a blue ribbon at the county fair last year; everyone swore they'd never tasted anything to touch it.

While Red had been out roaming the cold, muddy marshes, Jake had been home in the warm farmhouse kitchen, cooking all afternoon. There was catfish fried crisp and golden, as well as buttermilk biscuits oozing fresh creamy butter and dripping with honey. He had even cooked up some corn on the cob glistening yellow in the evening light. And in the middle of the table, towering over all this abundance, was Jake's prize winning chocolate layer cake.

Red grabbed a fork and stabbed a plump catfish.

"No," said Jake.

"No! What do you mean, *no?*" roared his brother.

"I mean," said Jake evenly, "that this is my supper, and you can't have it. Get your own supper."

"Aw, Jake," wheedled Esau, "there's more here than you can eat in a week. Let me have some. I'm so hungry that I think I'm gonna die. You've got plenty."

Jake appeared to think it over for a moment, then he said, "All right, you can have something to eat."

Esau let out a yell and grabbed a biscuit. He got it halfway to his mouth, when Jake stopped him once again.

"You can have something to eat . . . for a price. This food ain't free. You have to pay me for it."

"Anything," agreed Red, almost tasting the biscuit and butter and honey. "I'll pay whatever you want." He began to dig in his pockets. "How much do you want?"

"Just sign this paper. It says that when Daddy's gone, you give me all rights to your inheritance. The farm will come to me, not to you."

"Are you crazy?" boomed Red. "You know I can't sign no fool paper saying any such a thing!"

"Fine, then, don't sign." And Jake reached over and grabbed the biscuit out of his brother's hand.

"Take or leave it, that's the price of this meal." Jake cut a big old piece of the chocolate cake he knew was Red's favorite, and took a bite, keeping his eyes on his brother as he slowly chewed.

"Shoot," sputtered Red. "This farm ain't no use to me if I starve to death. Give me the darn paper. I'll sign." Esau scrawled his name across the bottom of Jake's paper, signing over his birthright. Red's great inheritance, gone for the price of a good meal.

The story goes on from there, one of the Bible's most dramatic, a story of trickery and deceit, love and reconciliation, power and conflict. But this little section ends with the cryptic judgment: "Thus did Esau despise his birthright." We also despise poor old Esau. How foolish and shortsighted, we think, to give up something as precious as his birthright for something as fleeting and meaningless as a full stomach. What a fool!

But aren't we all a little like Esau? Aren't we all willing to put our birthrights on the mark down table as well? For our birthright is the kingdom of God, and how often we have been willing to sell that for something much less enduring. How often we have been willing to put our fleeting wants above God's legitimate claim on our lives? How often, like Esau, have we been willing to sell our birthright as children of God in order to gratify an immediate want—a new car, a nice vacation, a slightly more comfortable lifestyle? When the time comes to make a financial commitment to God's work, all these things can seem a lot more important and necessary, much more urgent and critical than claiming our birthright as God's children.

Our congregation has a stewardship campaign every year for some practical reasons. We need to know about how much income to expect so we can do a responsible job of budgeting our expenditures for the coming church year. We need to let you all know in a fuller way what it costs in terms of dollars and cents to keep this church operating in the black. But true stewardship is about more than budgets and the bottom line, although too often we talk as if stewardship were only about writing a check or making a pledge. If all we need to do is balance the budget, then we're talking about fund-raising and finances, not Christian stewardship. Stewardship is about a lot more than finances.

I hope that each of us will see the next several weeks as a time to look inward, to re-examine our priorities and the values that guide how we spend our money and time and energy. I want us to reflect truthfully on the difference between what we say we value and what our actions say is important to us.

Our birthright is the kingdom of God. This kingdom comes to us because we are children of God. Our birthright comes to us as God's gracious gift, unmerited and unearned. Perhaps because it comes to us so freely, we, like Esau, tend to value it too cheaply. But while our birthright is absolutely free, it is not cheap. It is not a "K-Mart blue light special." We will not find it on the 75 percent off mark down table along with all the other out of season merchandise.

I don't think Esau really despised his birthright, in the way we usually think of that word. But I do think he took it for granted. I don't think he valued it as he should. I think he was willing to settle for short-term gratification instead of looking at the long-term consequences.

And I think any of us can fall into that same trap.

Esau was not a bad man, but he was a foolish man. He was shortsighted. His values were clearly misplaced. We are all a lot like Esau. We can be foolish and shortsighted and have our values in the wrong place. All too often we take our identity as children of God for granted and are willing to trade our birth right for some fleeting gratification.

It was only after Esau sold off his birthright that he began to truly learn its value. And that may also be true of us. It may only be after we have learned that all the trappings of a comfortable life don't guarantee contentment or serenity; only after we discover that a new car can't hold us when we cry, and a beautiful house can't silence our fears; only after we look for answers in our possessions and find only more questions; only then is it true that we may begin to understand how truly valuable our birthright really is.

An Analysis of René Jensen's "Birthright on the Mark Down Table"

René Jensen's sermon begins working the moment worshippers read her title in the bulletin. "Birthright on the Mark Down Table," instantly conjures everyday images of people hunting bargains. Unsurprisingly, when Jensen ties this bargain-hunting image to stewardship, her subsequent theological points arise in bold relief.

Jensen's sermon also works because she takes an ancient story and makes it contemporary. By using modern vernacular to tell the story of Esau and Jacob, Jensen matter-of-factly enables listeners to imagine that this kind of thing happens all the time. She makes listeners imagine that "Red" and "Jake" are like the people that the listeners know.

Some of the phrases she uses are good examples of rhetoric. Descriptive turns of phrase—"slicker than a greased pig on the Fourth of July," "they should count the fillings in their teeth," "who would take Mary Sue Barnes to the prom," "the best way to skin a deer"—each to engage the listeners. Thus, Jensen confers on this story fresh meaning for her hearers. If one of the purposes for preaching is to make the biblical texts come alive, then preachers can learn something from Jensen's inventive language and mode of communication.

Another excellent strategy Jensen employs to enliven her sermon is the use of dialogue. Certainly, preachers can merely summarize biblical conversations. Many of us do it routinely. Rather than rehash the old exchange between Esau and Jacob, however, Jensen refashions the conversation. By so doing she draws her congregation into the "He said, he replied" format. Thus, she animates what could have merely been a report on someone else's conversation.

This is an example of an effective sermon. It deals with a difficult and old story that seems distant from contemporary people. Most congregations today do not think of patriarchal blessings or birthrights. Yet, Jensen effectively closes the historical gap between this ancient story and modern people. She suggests that contemporary Christians need to remember what is truly important for building a life that is faithful to God's realm. She resourcefully identifies with the questions and compulsions of modern-day people. Overall, this is a highly helpful stewardship sermon. Alert preachers can learn much from Jensen's sermon gift.

CHAPTER THREE

"FIRST FRUITS"

Emery A. Percell

Emery A. Percell describes the context for this particular sermon:

"First Fruits" was a sermon given on "First Fruits Sunday," October 15, 2000, at Christ United Methodist Church in Rockford, Illinois. The Gospel reading was the lectionary for the day. During worship, the congregants saw a six-minute video portraying people of all ages engaged in church activities and outreach ministries. We also celebrated the sacrament of the Lord's Supper and people brought their commitment cards to the Lord's Table.

Over the past several years, pledged amounts have increased, but decreased in proportion to the total increase in giving. The First Fruits program has been a great way to increase our total giving by 25 percent over the last three years. It is a yearlong program of keeping the idea of giving and the needs of the church in front of people. One Sunday a month, there is a five-minute testimonial given in each service on the blessings of generous giving. Each month, a five-minute mission moment highlights part of the mission outreach in Rockford, in the Northern Illinois Annual Conference, or globally through United Methodist missions.

"First Fruits"

Mark 10:17-31

Of course, Jesus did not demand that everyone sell all they have and give the money to the poor; just this man who not only had many possessions but, in addition, wanted to "inherit" eternal life. Of him, Jesus demanded the giving of it all away. You have to admit that Jesus knew how to make a point!

The point was and is that Jesus calls disciples who are willing to leave everything to follow him. The point is that Christian discipleship is a total commitment of life to Jesus! We are not talking about religious professionals here. Whether you are a soccer mom or president of the company, Jesus calls you to make a total commitment of your life to follow him.

The man in our story was a good man. Yet he evidently sensed something lacking. He knew how to make money. He knew that moral living was important to his success. Eternal life, however, simply escaped him. "What must I do," he asked Jesus, "to inherit eternal life?" "You know the commandments," Jesus replied. " 'You shall not murder; You shall not commit adultery; You shall not bear false witness; You shall not defraud' . . . and you will have treasure in heaven."

Ah, yes, the man of many possessions was acquainted with all these. From the day Moses brought these directives down from Mt. Sinai, they have guided us through the wilderness of every generation. They are trustworthy and sure.

The inquirer had kept all of these commands from his youth. They still, however, had not been able to buy him a policy on eternal life. Admittedly, eternal life would be an unrealized benefit for many years. Yet, he would like some assurance that he could lock it up in his portfolio.

"Well, if you really want to get to the Promised Land of eternal life," Jesus replied, "there is one thing you must do: Sell all you have, give the money to the poor, and follow me!"

The man was stunned. Divest himself totally? Put it all into an irrevocable trust? How totally absurd!

You and I know, of course, that eternal life is a gift, as are all of life and all possessions. We know that even the ability to work and accumulate possessions is a gift. There is nothing one can *do* to earn Eternal Life. It is part of God's promise. It is a gift!

There is, however, a way. The way is to follow Jesus. That is the great truth of the gospel. It is a miraculous, life-changing truth. When we follow Jesus, whole new worlds of meaning and joy are opened up to us.

Peter got it, sort of. After the man of many possessions turned away, Peter began to say to Jesus, "Look, we have left everything and followed you." Jesus replied, "Truly I tell you, there is no one who has left father or children or fields for my sake and for the gospel, who will not receive a hundred fold now in this age, and in the future, eternal life—houses, brothers, sisters, mothers, and children and fields—even in persecution!" You give away your possessions in order to follow Jesus. They are returned hundredfold.

One business executive in our congregation told me that, as a Christian, he was able to see the priority of his family, his employees, and the needs of this community. He said he couldn't be happier. He knew the importance of the bottom line. He watched the figures closely. But, when he kept his priorities straight, the production figures and the income were always there. "I thank God every day," he said, "for all that has been given to me. It's more than I have ever given."

Isn't that what Jesus was talking about? When we follow Jesus by loving God with our whole self and our neighbors as ourselves,

God gives back life in all its fullness. It is not earned but, rather, received; the net earnings on family and friends and the common life in our community.

Following Jesus reorders our priorities and opens up the fullness of life and the qualities of eternal life even now. The future age starts when we follow Jesus! Not only that, but giving it all to Jesus is a sacramental experience as well.

Economics professor, David E. Klemm, of the University of Iowa, spoke recently of "material spirituality." Every material object, he said, points beyond itself. It is a mistake for us to think of all the things we own as ends in themselves. Every material possession points beyond itself to the love of the Creator who gave it. Every material possession has also the potential to convey that divine love through us to the world. Material possessions are sacramental. Their power is only fully experienced in giving. ("The Economics of It All," a lecture given at A Conference on Property and Possession in Social and Religious Life, sponsored by the Lilly Foundation and The University of Chicago Divinity School, October 26, 2000.)

"The earth is the Lord's," wrote the Psalmist (Psalm 24:1). All that we own is part of that spiritual totality. All our possessions are full of possibilities beyond our ownership. God invites us to make our generosity a sacramental act of grace through which, first of all, we reach out and participate in the abundance of eternal life. Second, God reaches in with love for us and for the world.

Unfortunately, those who accumulate possessions for their own sake miss the way, although they may keep all the moral law! Unfortunately, possessiveness permeates all of life. "Having" a spouse, "having" children, "having" relationships, "inheriting" eternal life—it's a dead-end path. Following Jesus, however, opens up the right way and helps us realize the sacred potential of all we own.

What a tragedy that the man of many possessions turned away from Jesus, shocked and grieving. Can you imagine the joy he would have experienced in watching young people grow because of the scholarships he had provided? Can you imagine the fulfillment in his life through the new library he built in his town? God might have given his life back to him hundredfold. He would have begun to receive the blessings of eternal life the moment he turned to follow Jesus. God could have filled his possessions with "material spirituality."

Jesus asks each of us to make a total commitment of our lives to him and to the gospel. He may not ask you to sell all you have. Generous giving, however, is always a part of what it means to follow Jesus. Christ's church helps you at that point.

That's what the business executive I mentioned earlier told me. I had thanked him for a generous gift to Christ's church, and he thanked me for the First Fruits program. Giving the First Fruits, he said, helps him keep his eye on Jesus while God's blessing enriches everything else.

First Fruits is a concrete, doable way for us to follow Jesus. We cannot go back to Galilee and follow Jesus around. We can, however, follow Jesus' love through the streets of Rockford this year. Christ's Church gives us a clear way to experience the sacramental power of our possessions. Christ's Church helps us read the map to Eternal Life.

We remind ourselves how wonderful it is to nurture each other in our biblical faith. We remind ourselves, as we did last Sunday, of the Rainbow Covenant missions through our United Methodist Church. Our First Fruit dollars follow Christ around the world. That is the priority that orders all the rest of life. The blessings flow through our gifts.

I want you now to think of your First Fruits—how Jesus is asking you to step out and follow him on the journey to eternal life. Neither I nor the Stewardship Committee, are here to tell you what you should give. You decide what is appropriate. Our long tradition of generous giving tells us, however, that your giving decision does have first priority. Listen for the spirit of the risen Christ to guide you in the sacramental generosity of your First Fruits.

The promise of God is out there before you:

There is no one who has left possessions and family and friends and self for Jesus' sake who will not receive a hundredfold now in this age, and in the age to come, eternal life.

An Analysis of Emery A. Percell's "First Fruits"

Emery Percell's sermon on "First Fruits" ties in nicely with the morning worship theme and the church's finance campaign. But Percell does more in this sermon than try to raise the church's budget. Rather, he helps people grasp a deeper understanding of authentic stewardship. Using the story of the man with many possessions from Mark's Gospel as his text, Percell allows a most expansive understanding of stewardship to bleed through. Percell defines stewardship as a believer's commitment to exercise discipleship.

In a very subtle way, Percell manages to portray the man with many possessions as more than a mere biblical caricature. He allows us to see the man as a real human being. One way he does this is by alluding to traits that modern people can readily imagine and even appreciate. For example, Percell writes that the man was good, knew how to make money, and considered moral living important to his success. Most modern Christians can identify with a person like this. For the listeners, this man becomes like us and, therefore, his dilemma can be our predicament as well. Percell makes it easy for us to relate to this man with many possessions. Compared to many of the people on this earth, we are people of many possessions, are we not?

A final note that merits mention is Percell's ability to use modern financial terms to help contemporary people relate to the ancient Bible from which we receive this story. When Percell uses terms like "material spirituality," "portfolio," "divest," and "an irrevocable trust," he demonstrates his familiarity with contemporary financial jargon. Thus, this sermon may resonate with even the most skeptical in the congregation. Overall, this sermon tells a biblical story well. It also makes stewardship pertinent to those who desire authentic discipleship in Jesus.

CHAPTER FOUR

"WITH GLAD AND GENEROUS HEARTS"

William H. Willimon

William H. Willimon describes the context for this particular sermon:

This sermon was preached on a Sunday after Easter when the first lesson, prescribed by the Common Lectionary, was Acts 2:42-27. In the days after Easter, it is good for the church to be reminded that the resurrection has practical, mundane, and material consequences. The church that believes in the resurrection must witness to the resurrection by the way its members live.

This is a teaching sermon, an attempt at explanation. It lifts up an act of worship—the Sunday offering—hoping that members will find new and fresh meaning. The sermon is a simple, straightforward commentary on an act of worship, a rationale for why we do what we do on a Sunday morning. In the sermon, a rather archaic, abstract word like "stewardship" is given practical application. The offering, the oblation of Christians, is claimed as a sign of something at the center of the Christian life. It is to be hoped that, through this didactic, pastoral commentary on a familiar act of worship, the congregation will find renewed and deeper meaning in what they do.

"With Glad and Generous Hearts"

Acts 2:42-47

I want to talk to you today about an act of worship that you might have not thought of as worship—the offering.

In the early church, the offering consisted of the people's gifts of bread and wine for the holy meal. After the service, leftovers were taken (in the words of early church father Justin Martyr) to "the orphans and the widows, and those who are needy because of sickness or other cause, and the captives, and the strangers who sojourn amongst us."[1]

I've heard people say that, in the age of plastic money, the charge card, computerized banking, and revolving credit, couldn't the church find a more efficient, less intrusive way of collecting its due?

People, please pay attention as the plate is being passed down the pew, and as people place their gifts in it. Pay attention as the Jones family comes forward when the offering is received, bringing the loaf of bread and the pitcher of wine for Holy Communion, for something very important is happening here. The offering is a significant statement of faith.

The persistent danger, the sacrilege against which we must be eternally vigilant, is the tendency to divorce Sunday worship from daily life. It is the danger that all our hymns, our anthems, our soft organ voluntaries, our poetic preachers, our beautiful churches might somehow conspire to turn worship into an event which has nothing to do with everyday life. Unless there is some link between our worship of God and junior's spilt cereal at breakfast, the boring routine at the office, the monthly collection of bills, and the cancer which will not heal, then our worship is not only irrelevant to human need but also unfaithful to the gospel of Jesus Christ.

Never think that Sunday worship is mostly a "spiritual" affair. Christianity is an incarnational faith, meaning "in the body." Jesus is here as a visible, tangible sign that God could truly love us only by coming "in the body," by becoming incarnate in a Jewish carpenter's son from Nazareth. There may be religions where practice is confined to what you do in some holy place, hermetically sealed from the stress and strain of everyday life. There may be religions in which things like political debate, bodily health, material well-being, and physical needs are irrelevant. Christianity is not one of those religions. Christianity offers us a Lord who comes, not to take us out of this world, but to give us a way to live in this world.

Every time we receive the offering, we are giving visible, tangible expression to the materiality of the Christian faith. We are lifting up ordinary things like bread, wine, and money and saying that because of the life, teachings, death, and resurrection of Jesus, these ordinary things take on new significance for us. In his ministry, Jesus was always taking the everyday stuff of life—seeds, birds, flowers, coins, lepers, children—lifting them up, setting them in the context of God's kingdom, and thereby giving them redemptive significance. After meeting Jesus and after listening to his stories, you can't walk by a hungry person, lift up a loaf of bread, pick a flower, or gaze into the eyes of a child quite the same way as you did before meeting him. Ours is an incarnational faith.

How many times have you felt that your minister was forever urging you to "get out there and do something" but never gave you anything specific to do?

Now, in the offering, it is your chance to do something. The offering is, in a way, the test of our worship. Is this service only a time to sing a few hymns, think a few lofty thoughts, feel a few warm fuzzies, and go home to a big meal? Or is this a time to put our money where our mouth is? Remember how Jesus noted that our hearts are usually where our money is and vice versa.

The offering isn't an unwarranted intrusion, it is the acid test of what we are about. It yokes our faith to our jobs, our daily cares and concerns, what we shall eat, what we wear, where we live, how we vote. We shouldn't apologize or be embarrassed by this act of worship, for it is an act that typifies the peculiar Christian stance toward the world, a stance typified by the person of Jesus himself.

Have you ever heard someone say, "I think that the main business of the church is to stick to saving souls and stay out of politics"?

"I think preachers should stick with theology and avoid controversial subjects like economics, business, or political matters."

"What a person gives or doesn't give is his or her own business."

"I'm tired of churches talking about nothing but money, money, money. They should be concerned with more spiritual matters."

How we wish it were so!

In a former church of mine, we were in a board meeting debating how to conduct the church's annual stewardship campaign. The discussion was becoming heated; emotions were beginning to boil. One member said, "I get so tired of all this talk about money. I hope that we can get this kind of thing out of the way and get on to more important church business—like religion!"

I responded, "Well, what is our business? Perhaps all this talk about money is not a religious matter. But don't you find it interesting that we have been meeting all year, discussing all manner of church business without even a mild argument? Yet, when we discuss money, suddenly everyone gets very heated. I have a feeling that we may at last be discussing *the* really big concern for most of us."

The offering is the link, the necessary connection between our intentions and our deeds, our spiritual impulses and our materialistic commitments. The offering reminds us that Christian worship is an ethical affair. A Christian does in church on Sunday that which he or she does Monday through Saturday in the world; namely, to offer their life to God. Our actions, our gifts, our deeds are our offering, our way of giving back to the God who has so graciously given to us.

Did you hear this note in our first lesson today, Acts 2:42-47? Acts says that, after Easter, at the end of Pentecost, the church gathered on a weekly basis in order to devote "themselves to the apostles' teaching and fellowship, to the breaking of bread and the prayers." That's us on Sunday, just like the first apostles at worship. Isn't that what we do on Sunday?

Yet the scripture continues: "All who believed were together and had all things in common; they would sell their possessions and goods and distribute them the proceeds to all, as any had need."

Note the link between worship in the church and their lives in the world, the way they linked economics to liturgics, Sunday to Monday.

You want to know the test of our worship? It's how "together" we are as the church; it's whether or not our worship of God in church is able to produce "glad and generous hearts" so that we are concerned about those in need.

It's not about how well we are able to listen to the word, or to sing the hymns. It's about how well we are able to show forth our gladness and generosity in offering ourselves and our gifts to God. Amen.

An Analysis of William H. Willimon's "With Glad and Generous Hearts"

"With Glad and Generous Hearts" is an effectively succinct "communion meditation" by well-known preacher Will Willimon. Willimon's effectiveness originates in his suggestion

that the Sunday offering is an act of worship. Like good preachers frequently do, Willimon reminds listeners of something they
previously recognize, but are prone to overlook. For example,
most people know that Christians are thankful people, yet the
Thanksgiving sermon is often difficult for preachers because the
act of thanksgiving is so widely accepted as a commonplace.
Good preachers strike a chord in us about the things we already
know but tend to forget. Willimon is shrewd enough to connect
the offering with another act of worship—the Eucharist—which
itself means "thanksgiving."

After the acknowledgement of the offering as an act of worship, he then reminds his congregation that we habitually sepa-
rate the spiritual from the mundane. Following this insight,
Willimon suggests that, because our faith is incarnational, the
spiritual resides in the mundane and the mundane in the spiritual. Willimon backs up this assertion with his meditation's most
telling sentence as he speaks of Jesus' incarnation: "Here is a Lord
who comes to us, not to take us out of this world but to give us a
way to live in the world."

In this meditation, Willimon offers an extended illustration
that not only is the offering an act of faith, but that our offerings
also incarnate our faith into daily life. In doing so, Willimon
relates the offering as an act of worship to individuals' daily lives.
For this reason alone this sermon is apt to connect with listeners.
One explicitly expressed congregational concern is for preachers
to show us how to get out there and do something. Willimon does
this admirably. This meditation connects the intention of the
believer to the deeds that Christ expects of us.

CHAPTER FIVE

"SAINTS ARE HARD TO FORGET"

J. Ellsworth Kalas

J. Ellsworth Kalas describes the context for this particular sermon:

This sermon was preached at the Centenary United Methodist Church in Danville, Kentucky, on November 7, 1999. They were celebrating All Saints Day, with the reading of the roll of their honored dead, and they were also in the midst of a month-long stewardship emphasis, so I sought to combine the two themes. From a pragmatic point of view, this had much to commend it because most stewardship efforts come at the season of All Saints. As the sermon began to unfold for me, I realized that the connection could not have been more appropriate.

"Saints Are Hard To Forget"

Acts 9:36-43

I'm old enough that I still think a long distance telephone call probably means bad news or at least an emergency. On this particular day, the voice at the other end of the line was appropriately urgent—pleasant, but urgent. It was an editor, telling me that my book was ready to go to press, except for one thing: they still needed my dedication page.

Dedication pages have always been difficult for me. It was easy as long as I stayed within the family, but when I began to branch out, I hardly knew where to start or to stop. It seems to me that I owe thanks to so many people for so many things and yet, to recognize one person often makes me fear that I will unintentionally hurt someone else. "I'll call back tomorrow," I said.

But I knew my answer almost before I hung up the phone. Hulda Weintz.

In so many ways, Hulda was a strange choice. She has been dead at least fifty years, and if I were to tell you how long it has been since I last saw her, I would only set your calculators going in an effort to estimate my age. Furthermore, because neither Hulda nor her sister Carrie ever married, there would be no one to recognize the tribute I might pay. So why did I want to dedicate a book to her and another friend?

I wanted to dedicate my book to Hulda because she was a saint, and saints are hard to forget. She came into my life when I was only ten years old, but I've never forgotten her. That's because she was a saint.

But first I'd better tell you what I mean by a saint. Actually, I mean what most of us probably mean when we speak of someone being a saint. I'm not using the New Testament definition. As the New Testament sees it, you and I and everyone else who chooses to follow Christ is a saint. In the New Testament view, I suppose you could say that we are all works in progress. I mean more than that, however, when I refer to Hulda Weintz, just as you probably do when you say that someone is a saint.

On the other hand, I'm not using the term the way the Roman Catholic Church does. In Catholicism's definition, a saint is someone who has been officially canonized by the church with proper certification by miracles and after examination by proper tribunals. Of course, the Catholic Church and most other Christian bodies recognize that many people may have qualified as saints without ever being officially designated. That's why we celebrate All Saints Day on November first.

No, I'm talking about saints the way you and I often do; that is, we call someone who is an especially fine person, "a real saint." No church authority has approved our judgment and we might be hard put to explain why we've chosen this person. We call someone a saint because we feel sentimental about them, or maybe because we have a longing for more good people in the world, so we do our own canonizing in order to fill the void.

But I know why Hulda was a saint. In truth, it was for the same reason a woman named Dorcas would also qualify as a saint.

Let me tell you about Dorcas. We read her story as our text of the morning, but since not many are familiar with Dorcas, our story will bear some reviewing. In truth, it's easy to lose her story. It is tucked in rather inconspicuously between two really big events. Chapter nine of Acts tells the story of the conversion of Saul of Tarsus, who becomes Paul, the apostle. He is one of the three or four most important figures in the New Testament, so his conversion is eternal headline news. The next chapter is the story of Cornelius, the first non-Jew to come into the early Christian Church. In a sense, the story of Cornelius is the hinge on which the rest of the history of the Christian Church will swing.

And between those two stories comes Dorcas. No wonder she doesn't get more attention!

So who was Dorcas? She has two names—Tabitha in Aramaic, and Dorcas in Greek. Both names mean the same thing: gazelle. This is a pretty name, giving one the feeling that she may have been an attractive woman. Names are important in that way. She was a disciple of our Lord. I wish I could tell you that most disciples are like her. But, unfortunately, that isn't the case. The Bible says that she was "devoted to good works and acts of charity" (Acts 9:36). All Christians ought to be like that, but it doesn't always happen that way.

Now probably all of us here are pretty good people, so you may be patting yourself on the back just now, feeling that you are a kind of twenty-first century Dorcas. But there's more. Dorcas became ill and died, suddenly and without warning. They bathed her body in preparation for burial. But then someone mentioned that the apostle Peter was only a few miles away. So they sent two men to Peter. "Come without delay," they said.

And Peter did. For us it would be a long walk—some eleven miles. But they were accustomed to walking in those days, so Peter and his companions struck out toward the place where Dorcas' body lay in state. When Peter arrived, he found an interesting mourning party: a large group of widows, all of them weeping, and all of them anxious to show him "tunics and other clothing that Dorcas had made while she was with them" (Acts 9:39).

What kind of woman was Dorcas? She was someone who made clothing to give to the poor—especially to the widows. Widows were the most helpless people in that first century world; they depended almost entirely on the kindness of others because they usually had no sure means of support. Dorcas apparently was a pretty fair seamstress, and either she had enough money to buy cloth, or she begged it from others. In any event, she was constantly making clothing for those widows who were otherwise neglected. So when she died, all of these women knew that their most dependable and helpful earthly friend was gone. They were devastated.

Well, the Bible says that Peter knelt down and prayed, then turned to the dead body and said, "Tabitha, get up." She opened her eyes and, when she saw Peter, she sat up. It was a miracle! Just in passing, let me say this. I give full credit to the remarkable faith and prayers of Peter, but I have a feeling that the weeping and the love of the widows mightily assisted his prayers.

The first century world was tough. They didn't have miracle drugs, modern medical procedures to lengthen life, or painkillers to ease the approach of death. They faced death at close hand, not through the remoteness of hospitals. Death was real and near for them; they expected it and learned to go on after it invaded their lives. But when Dorcas died, death seemed to have a different face. They couldn't let Dorcas go. She was a saint, and saints are hard to forget.

Why do I call her a saint? The Bible tells us nothing about her prayer life or her personal character, and we have no evidence that she was even a student of the scriptures.

But this we know—Dorcas was a giver. She was constantly giving her time, her ability, and her resources. Saints are always givers. Can you imagine describing someone as a "stingy saint?" The two words simply don't go together; they're the ultimate oxymoron. If there is any one thing that inevitably characterizes a saint, it is that he or she is a giver, a big-time giver!

And that brings me back to Hulda Weintz. She was a giver. Hulda didn't belong to the little Methodist Church my family attended; she spent her Sundays at the Helping Hand Mission, a rather nondescript church on lower Fourth Street. Helping Hand was the kind of church you might expect from its name. It was a rescue mission seven nights a week and, on Sundays, a church for a few faithful families and whoever else appeared. The Sunday school was almost entirely comprised of children whose parents had no relationship to the church. As a result, the mission was always short of Sunday school teachers. Hulda Weintz belonged to another church, but came to the mission every Sunday to teach a class. On the whole, the facilities weren't very impressive, but Hulda taught it faithfully. She was a giver.

In those days, little boys often made a few pennies by selling magazines from door to door, and I do mean *pennies!* If you sold four *Liberty* magazines, you made a nickel; if you sold something like a *Delineator* or a *Pictorial Review*, you made four or five cents on just one sale. It was no way to get rich, but it was the only kind of income available, other than picking up rags or bottles. But of course not many people wanted to buy the magazines, so one went from door to door without much hope. I was a particularly inept salesman, so my hopes were especially low. But my mother would advise at intervals, "Go to Hulda and Carrie Weintz. They'll buy one from you." And they always did. I'm not at all sure that they wanted the magazines. But they were giving people.

Hulda was my Sunday school teacher at the time I gave my life to Christ. One day she explained to the boys in our Sunday school class that Christians should tithe; that is, that we should give ten percent of everything we earned, or money that someone gave us, to the work of the Lord. It never occurred to me to argue the point. I was ten years old and a new Christian, and I knew that Hulda Weintz was a wonderful human being. If this was the way she lived, giving a tenth of her income to God, and she said we ought to do the same thing, I knew this was the way to go.

So I began tithing because Hulda Weintz recommended it, and I've been doing so ever since. This makes me tremendously indebted to her. Wouldn't you feel indebted to someone who urged you to buy a piece of property for five thousand dollars and, in a few years, it became worth several million dollars? Well, that's the way I feel about Hulda teaching me to tithe. She has made my soul a multimillionaire. She gave me a real sense of the value of a dollar. I learned that a dollar is more than something with which you can buy food, clothing, furniture, a house, a car, and stocks and bonds. It is also—and far more importantly—something with which you can invest in eternity.

So that's why I can't forget Hulda Weintz—she was a saint, and saints are hard to forget. And how do I know that she was a saint? Because she was a giver! She gave time, love, talent, simple caring, and money. Last summer, when I was back in my hometown of Sioux City, Iowa, I walked the street to see if I could still recognize her house. I discovered that it wasn't much of a house, at most, a modest bungalow. But I knew it was worth pausing for a moment at it, to think again about the debt I owe this saint.

Often when people speculate thoughtfully on their lives, they'll say, "When I die, I just hope I will be remembered. I hope people will think of me kindly." I'm here to tell you that it's really rather easy. If you want to be remembered, be a *giver*. Give God and people your time, your money, your love, and your ability—they will remember you because you'll be a saint, and saints are hard to forget. That's why the people in Joppa couldn't let Dorcas die. And that's why I remember Hulda Weintz.

An Analysis of J. Ellsworth Kalas's "Saints Are Hard to Forget"

Few pastors can relate to people in the pew like Ellsworth Kalas does without sacrificing preaching that is both deeply biblical and thoughtfully theological. As a preacher, Kalas inspires people to embrace the gospel's expectations of them. This sermon showcases Kalas' relational abilities with listeners.

Kalas begins by putting a human face on stewardship. For many believers, stewardship is a theological code word for "money." Yet, Kalas' sermon opening disarms even the most skeptical listeners. Using the qualities of Hulda Weintz, his former Sunday School teacher, he portrays a faithful saint—and then defines "saint." By defining what a saint is and is not, Kalas guides listeners to a deeper appreciation of authentic saintly qualities.

After drawing the congregation in and defining "saint," Kalas then concentrates on the biblical text. By comparing and contrasting Dorcas (or Tabitha) to Hulda Weintz, he uses a longstanding rhetorical formula. This rhetorical ploy also helps the congregation connect an ancient biblical character to a more contemporary person with whom the congregation can confidently imagine. Kalas sets the context of Dorcas' ministry and then draws analogies to contemporary acts of discipleship.

The sermon's climax arrives when Kalas asks: "Why do I call her a saint?" He then clarifies the trait of being "a giver." It is this attribute that sets Dorcas apart and why we remember her as a saint. Giving is part of the definition of a saint. Coming full circle, Kalas then relates Hulda Weintz's life to the discipleship of Dorcas. Kalas also carefully weaves Hulda Weintz's specific gift to him into the sermon—she taught him to tithe. He even implies the impact of this gift by saying, "She has made my soul a multi-millionaire." By sermon's end, Kalas gives this congregation several memorable characters to take with them. He also inspires them to go and do likewise.

CHAPTER   SIX

"Generosity"

Robert A. Hill

Robert A. Hill describes the context for this particular sermon:

One of the toughest challenges of the stewardship sermon lies in the nearly unavoidable temptation to forget the gospel as the sermon is prepared. James Sanders tried to teach us to "theologize first, then moralize." Remembering his wisdom can be a challenge in preaching about stewardship.

This sermon was preached in the course of a series of nine sermons in the Fall of 1999. The series interpreted Galatians 5:22ff, "the fruit of the Spirit." The particular word in Greek has a rich history, well explored in J. L. Martyn's *Galatians* (Anchor Bible Commentary). I invited the congregation to consider whether divine generosity may affect the church. The tone is meant to be joyful, the manner playful, the content biblical, the argument traditional.

Asbury First United Methodist Church in Rochester has a membership of 2,200, a worshipping attendance of 900, an annual financial plan of $1.2 million, a benevolence budget of $170,000, and additional annual mission giving of $90,000.

"Generosity"

Galatians 5:22

Prayer: O Lord, give us an appetite for the fruit of your spirit, we pray. We ask today, especially, for a taste of generosity—surprising, spacious, seductive generosity. Amen.

We savor, today, what the scripture names as the Spirit's fruit—goodness or, perhaps better rendered, "generosity;" goodness that does some good, generative goodness, *agathosune*, generosity.

This is the day, either literally or figuratively, in which another reality invades, assaults, attacks the material world. The beachhead of this invasion is unmistakable, as real and sacrificial and human and costly—and victorious—as Normandy.

Tom Brokaw has written about *The Greatest Generation*. Tom Hanks has starred in *Saving Private Ryan*. But that kind of beachhead, won against frightful gunfire and destructive opposition, is also visible every November even in the lowliest church and the poorest parish. It goes simply by the name of generosity. Generosity is a surprising interloper, a fruit of God's Spirit, a visitation from another reality. With the enemy fire raining down, generosity marches on.

Into the teeth of congenital selfishness, cultural stinginess, communal exclusiveness, and congregational sanctimoniousness, generosity marches on.

Into the terror of rational questioning, too, generosity advances. "You can't give like that now, you're just getting started. You shouldn't do that, you have little mouths to feed.

Now is not the time, you are paying a mortgage. How can you give with kids in college? Better save now, your hair is receding and so is your bank balance. Your teeth are decaying and so is your portfolio. Your stomach is growing and so is your debt. Your eyesight is fading and so are your options. You'll need resources as you get older." Against all that, generosity moves forward, into the teeth of the gale, and the fierce enemy fire from hidden outposts.

But what is the character of the fruit of the Spirit known as generosity? How shall we know its taste in this season of spiritual harvest?

An Apocalyptic Moment

Last month I did have a Sunday off. What a luxury! We were in Phoenix, with sunshine and 100 degree heat. I got up late, skipped breakfast, went to a worship service someone else had prepared, ate lunch, and headed out to see if I could get into a professional football game—the Cardinals and Giants. I have followed the Giants since the days of Y. A. Tittle, Del Shoefner, and Frank Gifford. However, I had never seen them live. So I went to the stadium and worried about getting a ticket. Some scalpers had tickets for $100 dollars. No thank you! At last I arrived at the ticket booth, where a little crowd had gathered. I stood and waited in line.

Suddenly, a Phoenix fan appeared dressed in a Cardinals hat, a Cardinals shirt, Cardinals socks, and Cardinals buttons. He was a burly bloke and not overly tidy in his attire. He was also quite a large person. He wore a beverage container on his back that had a tube running to his mouth. His Cardinals hat was shaped like a bird, and had wings that moved up and down as if it were in flight as he walked. He wore what looked to be size 13 Converse sneakers. He stood in the ticket area and said, "I have two $50 tickets that I want to give away. I don't want to sell them. I want to give them away."

No one moved. No one spoke.

"I have free tickets here—two of them. They're on the 30-yard line, 18 rows up. I want to give them away."

I don't know why, exactly, but no one moved or spoke. We couldn't believe it. "There must be something wrong, some kind of a catch," we all thought. Finally, exasperated, Mr. Cardinal slammed his tickets on the counter, and said to the ticket vendor, "You give them away!" At which point yours truly, not born yesterday, said, "Well, I appreciate your generosity—thanks for the tickets. May the best team win as long as it's New York."

We don't really appreciate generosity. We don't expect it so we don't see it. It stomps up to us and bites us and we still don't see it. I was given a place at the table, a seat at the banquet, a ticket to the game—space, entrance, inclusion.

So armed, I walked to the turnstile and realized I had two tickets but only needed one. So, I walked over to a group nearby and said, "Listen, I have a free ticket here. I don't want it scalped. Who would like it?"

Guess what? Dead silence.

"Hey. This is legitimate. Because someone gave me the ticket I want to give it away. It's yours—for free." Nothing.

I turned to leave, when an older man said, "OK, OK, I don't know what your angle is, buddy, but hand it over." I did so.

So, on a 100 degree Sunday off in the southwest, I was given a free ticket and, as the game progressed and my mind wandered, an apocalyptic insight into the nature of the fruit of the Spirit known as generosity, in three particulars.

- Generosity surprises us.
- Generosity makes space for others, especially for the stranger, the outsider, the other.
- Generosity seduces us, at last, into offering our own generous gifts.

Generosity Surprises Us

For example, an elderly couple who met at DePauw University in 1926, but never graduated, decide to leave that school their entire life savings—$128 million dollars. Seventy-five students a year will attend that school with full scholarships. Surprising generosity.

A person visits our church office and, later that week, mails our church a check for $3,000, for us to use as we "see fit." Surprising generosity.

The work of this church's Dining Center inspires a woman who does not attend our church to leave that ministry a quarter of a million dollars. Surprising generosity. May her tribe increase.

A family needs a place to stay for a summer trip and, hearing the need, a brother in Christ provides a home for the visit. Surprising generosity.

A president is defeated at the polls after only one term, but goes on to live a faith both public and private—the Carter Center, Jimmy Carter's post-presidential agency for peace and justice, thrives. Surprising generosity.

It is in the nature of the Spirit to take us somewhat by surprise and nourish us generously. So the scriptures teach us.

Psalm 33:5: The earth is full of the *hesed* (generous goodness) of the Lord.

Matthew 5:40: If anyone asks for your coat, give him your cloak as well. If he asks you to go one mile, go a second one too.

Romans 12:6, 8: We have gifts . . . the giver gives in generosity.

Romans 12:9: Let love be genuine.

2 Corinthians 9:7: The Lord loves a cheerful giver.

Galatians 6:2: Bear one another's burdens and so fulfill the law of Christ.

Galatians 6:10: Let us be generous to all.

Colossians 1:10: Be fruitful in every good work.

Or think of Jesus' parables of sowing and reaping, of mustard seeds exploding from tiny to great, of talents used and underused, of dishonest but generous stewards, and of that haunting and joyous refrain—may it reach our ears at heaven's door! "Well done, thou generous and faithful servant; you have been faithful over a little, we will set you over much. Enter into the joy of the master" (paraphrase of Matthew 25:23). How frightful, daunting, awesome, and profound is our charge in this life to minister to one another so that we are ready to hear such a sentence pronounced: "Well done, thou generous and faithful servant."

If we have savored generous surprise, then we may also sense that this form of the Spirit's fruit makes space for others.

Generosity Makes Space for Others

Look at Asbury First, flourishing because of the surprising generosity of hundreds of faithful people. These are people who want the world to be a better place, who believe in the Lord Jesus Christ, who understand that as the seedbed for wonder, morality, and future generosity, the church has a prior claim on our giving.

Let me push you a little here. I know it is appealing to give to many particular causes and special projects. But it is another reality, the fruit of God's own spirit known as goodness, which ultimately feeds all giving and to which the church alone bears full witness. I think we run the risk of taking our church for granted. It will prevail into the new millennium only to the degree that another generation of young adults learns and chooses to reflect divine generosity with some of the human variety.

One day a veteran member of our church made a comment to me about our ministry. In conclusion, she said, "We don't want anyone left behind." The words carried a depth of meaning beyond her intention.

That's it! No one is to be left behind, left out, left off the list, left outside. Not for those of us who worship the Jesus Christ of the manger, the wilderness, the borrowed upper room, the cross, and the empty tomb! Jesus lived and died "outside" to remind us of the religious inside—of those still outside so that all might have space, have a seat, have a place at the table. You and I have had seven courses of faith, when others lack even the appetizer.

Asbury First's current growth and future health are fed by generosity, goodness that does good. Generosity makes space, in this church, for those who are not yet inside. Why? Why more? Why grow? Because God is generous, and we believe in God. Because the need of the county is great, and we care about that need. The future health of this congregation depends on our becoming, welcoming, inviting, and generous. We want a healthy and inviting church most of all because we love this church. When our own generosity is quickened, faith is less a dull habit and more a burning passion.

Amid surprise and extra space, the Spirit can seduce you, even on a Stewardship Sunday.

Generosity Seduces Us

We learn over time. Sometimes the best gift you can give somebody is the opportunity for him or her to give of themselves. That is what this sermon is about. We are trying today, in this season of spiritual harvest, to feast upon the fruit of the Spirit known as generosity. The best gift you can receive is the chance to give of yourself.

A short time ago, some of our friends were going on a trip and needed someone to watch their children. I heard the request and did what you would have done—I referred the idea to the spiritual leader of our home. My wife said, "Sure." I wondered a little about it, but the day came and, all of a sudden, we again had multiple teenage voices in our home. What a treat they were, what a joyful presence, what a gift!

But what if our friends had not had the courage and taken the risk of asking, of giving us the real gift of a chance to give? Then we would have missed a little bit of heaven.

So, in that vein, I am going to ask you to give today. This church can prosper if you will generously support it. It's entirely up to you. I invite you to give, to pledge, to pledge strongly, and to tithe. I am aware that this is a very personal decision. Not everyone likes to hear, let alone preach, a stewardship sermon. One wag said, "It's not that he preaches so badly about money, it's that he preaches about it at all!"

Nevertheless our token pledges and convenient giving will not heal our world.

This is a giving church. It needs to become a generous one. That is your opportunity today. "Ask not what your church can do for you. Ask what you can do for your church."

Remember your forebears. These are the people Diognetus described in the year 130 C.E.:

> They display to us their wonderful and paradoxical way of life.
> They dwell in their own countries, but merely as sojourners.
> Every foreign land is to them their native country.
> And yet their land of birth is a land of strangers.
> They marry and beget children, but they do not destroy their offspring.
> They have a common table, but not a common bed.
> They are in the flesh, but they do not live after the flesh.
> They pass their days on earth, but they are citizens of heaven.
> When reviled, they bless.
> When insulted, they show honor.
> When punished, they rejoice.
> What the soul is to the body, they are to the world.
> What salt is to earth and light is to world, are you to this country, to this region.[1]

The church stays open for people on whom almost all other doors have closed. For the poor. For the irascible. For the difficult. You are sitting in the most open and generously vulnerable public space in this county.

Do you remember Lorraine Hansberry and what she wrote?

When do you think is the time to love somebody most?
When they done good and made things easy for everybody? Well then, you ain't through learning, because that
ain't the time at all. It's when he's at his lowest and can't
believe in himself 'cause the world done whipped him so.[2]

The mission may be the bit and bridle, but the the real horse-
flesh of life is found in a vision of a healed and loving world,
where there is space, real quality space, for all. We dare not let
the moon of mission eclipse the sun of vision.

Now we sing:
>Take my life and let it be
>Consecrated Lord to thee

We might better sing:
>Take my life and let it be
>Shaped by generosity.

Jane Addams' Warning

In closing, maybe we need to remember the young woman
from Rockford, Illinois—Jane Addams. She grew up 130 years
ago, in a time and place that was unfriendly, even hostile, to the
leadership that women might provide. But somehow she discovered her mission in life. With determination she traveled to the
windy city and set up Hull House, the most far-reaching experi-
ment in social reform American cities had ever seen. Hull House
was born out of a social vision, and nurtured through the generosity of one determined woman. Addams believed fervently
that we are responsible for what happens in the world. So Hull
House, a place of feminine community and exciting spiritual
energy, was born. Addams organized female labor unions. She
lobbied for a state office to inspect factories for safety. She built
public playgrounds and staged concerts and cared for immigrants.

She became politically active and gained a national following on the lecture circuit. She is perhaps the most passionate and effective advocate for the poor that our country has ever seen.

Addams wrote: "The blessings which we associate with a life of refinement and cultivation must be made universal if they are to be permanent . . . . The good we secure for ourselves is precarious and uncertain, is floating in midair, until it is secured for all of us and incorporated into our common life."[3]

Yet it was a Rochesterian who, for me, once explained the puzzle of Jane Addams' fruitful generosity. This was the historian Christopher Lasch. Lasch wrote of Addams, "Like so many reformers before her, she had discovered some part of herself which, released, freed the rest."

Is there a part of your soul ready today to be released that then will free the rest of you?

I wonder, frankly, whether for some of us that part is our stewardship life, our financial generosity.

Is that part of you, the wallet part, ready to be released today, and in so doing, to free up the rest?

I think with real happiness over the years of men who have, just for one example, taken up the practice of tithing, and in so releasing themselves, have found the rest of their lives unleashed for God.

Deep, real life change comes from apocalyptic insight and cataclysmic experience. All who enter the kingdom of heaven enter it violently (Matthew 11:12).

A sensual experience can reorient a life (Pablo Picasso's life experience shaped his artistic *oeuvre*, and the various biographies of Picasso illuminate this connection). A religious experience can reorient a life (Ignatius of Loyola, who founded the Jesuit order in 1540, did so as a consequence of his earlier trip to the Holy Land). A patriotic experience can reorient a life (John McCain's imprisonment in North Vietnam, while tragic and excruciating, gave form to his current public leadership). A near-death experience can reorient a life (Christopher Reeve, whose fictional portrayal of Superman impressed so many, may nonetheless have had more heroic impact in the wake of his tragic accident).

Sex, religion, patriotism, and death can all produce such a cataclysmic release. All are sticks of existential dynamite. Money, of course, is another. Today is Stewardship Sunday. I wonder about the verve and youthful zest of your lower wallet area? As the song says, I wonder "what condition your condition is in."

Is there a part of your soul which, once released, would free up the rest? A catalytic experience or moment? Is it possible that such an experience is waiting for you, metaphorically speaking, in the lobby outside your bank? Not in sex or religion or nation or peril, but in generosity?

Meryl Streep reminds us that music brings structure, focus, and discipline to life. So does tithing, and more so.

Maybe we can know, in the surprise of generosity, in the space provided by generosity, in the seductive attraction of generosity, what made a man of God out of John Wesley and helped him to live on a mere 60£ Sterling year by year for his whole adult life. In the process, he build a cross-continental movement for good, of which we are heirs and debtors. Go, tithers and future tithers, and live Wesley's motto:

> . Do all the good you can
> At all the times you can
> In all the ways you can
> In all the places you can
> To all the people you can
> As long as ever you can

An Analysis of Robert A. Hill's "Generosity"

Of all the sermons in this collection, Robert Hill's "Generosity" is clearly the most "oral," with René Rodgers Jensen's "Birthright on the Mark Down Table" running a close second. I have not edited these sermons to a great extent because it may be important for readers to see (and almost hear) how Hill and Jensen's messages look and "feel" on paper. Beyond the orality of Hill's text, however, there is a startling discovery. As we read this sermon, it impresses one as being something like an "All You Can Eat" smorgasbord.

"Generosity" appears to be a banquet for listeners whose homiletic appetites have been whittled downward from the sixty-minute sermon of yesteryear to the fashionable ten-minute "sermonette" that passes for preaching in many congregations today.

Clearly, length does not constitute the controlling factor in sermons. Yet in this sermon, Hill offers us much more than we can readily digest. His range of illustrative material runs from Y. A. Tittle to Tom Brokaw, from Tom Hanks and Meryl Streep to Jane Addams and Ignatius of Loyola. But I suspect that, although this particular sermon may stretch even the hardiest listeners, Hill knows his audience. This knowledge is vital to preachers. Some congregations need intellectual challenge, while others need to feel the message. Hill must understand the limits of a congregation's listening ability and therefore preaches at a level that suits their capacity. Aristotle cautioned ancient rhetors that one of the keys to effective rhetoric was to know the audience. Hill demonstrates that his audience is engaged in the preaching act.

This sermon illustrates above all else that pace is important in preaching. Hill varies his tempo from section to section. By inserting a personal story about a football game to illustrate the surprise of someone else's generosity, he thereby prepares his listeners for "an appeal to the will" portion of the sermon. This sermon asks much of its listeners, but provides them ample reason to respond to the challenge.

CHAPTER SEVEN

"A TIGHT SQUEEZE"

John C. Holbert

John C. Holbert describes the context for this particular sermon:

I preached this sermon in a most difficult context. I was interim minister of a 11,000 member United Methodist Church, whose previous pastor of 18 years had been removed from the pulpit while being investigated for sexual harassment. Many in the congregation simply could not believe that there was any substance to these charges and were furious at the hierarchy of the church, and at me, for taking their beloved leader away. Some of them made their anger clear by withholding their pledge monies. The church (with a $5,000,000+ budget) was in a very serious financial free-fall. This sermon began the Fall Financial Campaign.

"A Tight Squeeze"

Mark 10:17-31

The text of the day is from the Gospel of Mark. It is a famous and familiar story, but I want to go back through it in a different way to demonstrate what I think is an important element concerning the issue of stewardship.

Let us pray:

O God, speak through these words this day to our hearts. Open our hearts wide to hear the power of your grace, to feel your healing teaching, so that we become one with you and one with each other. In the name of Jesus the Christ, we pray. Amen.

Well, it is time again to think about stewardship. Now notice, I did not say it is time to think about money. I said it is time to think about stewardship and those are different things. As a matter of fact, I want to maintain today that stewardship is a more inclusive term and, in the long run, a much more important one. Stewardship. That is what we are about today.

This reminds me, as usual, of stories, and two come from the Gospel of Mark. There is the one I read to you just a moment ago, and then there is the one that immediately precedes it in Mark's Gospel, the story of Jesus' blessing of children. Why does Mark put these two stories together?

One of the things that is interesting about reading the Gospels is the way they are put together. This is a very important key to what they mean. They are not just individual stories plunked together in some sort of haphazard way. No, each Gospel writer puts them together in an exacting way to say particularly important things. One might argue that the Gospels themselves are sermons. I think Mark is a long narrative sermon about discipleship. And, in this case, it is about what disciples do as stewards.

Let me remind you of that story about the children. One day, as Jesus was teaching as he did regularly, some parents brought their children to him. Well, the disciples did not like it. The Greek text says they spoke sternly to the parents. They were angry with them. They didn't want Jesus to waste his time with these little children. Children in the first century were not very seriously considered. For Jesus to spend his time with the children was simply wasting precious teaching time for the adults. Jesus was very angry indeed. As a matter of fact, the Greek text says he was indignant. It is the only time in the Gospels where Jesus is indignant with his disciples; angry enough and stern enough to tell them where to get off. "Oh, what is the matter with you guys? Don't stop these children from coming. Don't hinder the children, of all people." "Well, why not?" the disciples ask. "Because, you see, to such as these belongs the kingdom of God." That is an astonishing thing for Jesus to say in the first century. Surely children do not belong in the kingdom of God. "Oh yes," says Jesus. Well, what does that statement mean?

I think the key word is dependence. Children are dependent for their lives and their livelihood on those who are older: parents, relatives, friends. They really cannot do many things on their own. They simply must be helped all of the time. Jesus says, "Unless you become like one of those, you will never even see the kingdom of God, let alone get into it. I mean, you won't even understand it at all unless you can open yourself enough, like a child, to be dependent on God. Without that, you will never see God's rule in your life." It is a very straightforward statement.

A few words about this "kingdom of God" business might be useful. Many people think differently about what the "kingdom of God" means. Some think it means what happens after you die. But the New Testament is much richer in its proclamation than that. Most of the time in the New Testament, the "kingdom of God" means the rule of God in life. We need not wait until we die to find that. One can see God's ruling in life while one is very much alive. Jesus says, "If you become like a child, dependent, really dependent for your gifts on God, you have a chance to see the kingdom of God in your own life. It's possible."

Well, that seems simple enough, all right. But then, right after that small message is taught, the next story comes up, the one we read earlier today. Jesus leaves the children behind with the parents and goes off down the road with the disciples in tow. And then something very interesting happens. Jesus meets a man. He is a rich man, it says. In the other Gospels, he is described as a rich young ruler. But here he is simply described as a rich man. A rich man, it says, ran up to him. Ran to Jesus—a remarkable thing for a dignified person in the ancient world to do. To run in the ancient world was simply not done by a person of dignity. But this man ran. He ran up to Jesus and, it says, he knelt. Kneeling in some kind of reverence or awe of Jesus, he says, "Good teacher." He starts his speech. Well, that seems innocuous enough to us, because we think of the word "good" in very general terms. But in the ancient world, to call somebody "good" was to say something quite remarkable. It was to claim that the person was almost divine or, at the very least, holy.

"Good teacher," says the man, "what must I do to inherit eternal life?" It is a very interesting phrase. Did you hear the way he put it? "What must I do?" Isn't it remarkable that this man asks that question directly after Jesus tells us in the preceding story that there is *nothing* we can do to inherit the kingdom. We must be dependent if we are going to see the kingdom. Now this man, in exactly contrary ways, asked Jesus some questions—"What must I do to inherit eternal life? How can I be certain that I will find my way to paradise? Can you tell me where I can buy a one-way ticket to the Promised Land? That is all I want."

These are very suspicious statements. Jesus is immediately suspicious. He says, "Why do you call me 'good' anyway?" Jesus says the man has really gone too far. "You think that there is some magic key by which you are going to find your way into the kingdom? That, if you could just do enough things, you'll find your way? Besides, are you trying to butter me up with that business about being good? You know perfectly well there is only one being that is good, and that is God. God is the only good one."

"Besides," he says, "you know the commandments, don't you?" Ah, now the rich man was on good ground. Being a good Jew, he certainly knew the commandments. Jesus lists some of them for him.

Well, now the rich man is on familiar ground. He knows these commandments. And he is thinking to himself, no doubt, "Oh good, is that all you have to do? Just follow those command-ments? Why heavenly days, I have done that all my life! Oh, goody, goody, goody, a one way ticket to paradise, here it comes!" And he says, no doubt with a great smile on his face, "I have done those from my youth," probably raising his hand like a child in class. I know the answer, teacher. I have done that all the time.

Jesus looked at him, the text tells us, and in a little line in verse twenty-one it says, "he loved him." That is very important. Jesus loved the rich man, and said, "Well, you know, you only lack one thing. Just one." The man was all ears. He wanted to know what could possibly be needed from him to inherit eternal life. Just one thing, just one. Listen to the verbs. "Go," says Jesus, "Sell what you own, give the money to the poor, and then you will have treasure in sheaven. Then come and follow me." Go and sell and give and come and follow—five rather shocking verbs. Well, when the rich man heard that, he was shocked. It was much more than that; he was appalled, he was astounded, he was horrified, and he went away grieving, weeping, and very sad indeed. Because, you see, he was really very rich.

Now this story is always troublesome, isn't it? Heavenly days. How often have we heard about Jesus asking the rich man to sell all he has? Now the question what we are we going to do about it. Every person in this sanctuary today, I mean all of us, bar none, is, by any standard of the world, very rich indeed. We don't have to know much to know that. We are a very rich people, rich in goods. We have freedom to do what we want, go where we want, buy what we want. Nobody can deny that. But if we limit the moral of this story to only giving away the goods, most of us won't do it, and the rest of us will feel guilty.

My claim here is that there is something much more at stake than that. It is not just a question of whether we are going to give away our money. It is a much more comprehensive problem that Jesus addresses, and he goes on to do that with his disciples. Jesus, after speaking to the rich man and watching him go down the road weeping, unwilling to follow, says this to the disciples. "I tell you, my friends, how hard it will be for those who have wealth to enter the kingdom of God. How difficult it will be, because sometimes your wealth gets in the way," he says. "It just gets in the way. It encumbers you, you live your life by it or for it. It is impossible, it is hard." And the disciples, you see, just like us, were very perplexed by these words, and Jesus said to them again, "Now look, children." Notice how he calls them children, the same word he uses in the story of the little children. "Children, look," he says , "how hard it is to enter the kingdom of God. You know it is easier for a camel to go through a needle's eye, than for a rich person to get into the kingdom of God."

Now we have heard all that before, haven't we? The early church heard this, too, and they didn't like it much, and couldn't imagine Jesus would have said something as silly as that. Good heavens! A camel through a needle's eye? This is crazy. So they made up some things that tried to make it easier to swallow. In the third century, one person who read this text changed the Greek word "camel" to the word "rope," which is pretty close with only one letter difference. He thought that if it was a rope, it might be a little easier to get through that needle's eye. No, that is not really going to help, is it? And then in the ninth century, another enterprising and creative scholar read this text and said, "Well, I know what it is. You see, the needle's eye is really not a needle's eye. It is really one of the gates to Jerusalem. So what Jesus was talking about was a fully loaded camel trying to get through this needle's eye." That is all very interesting, but there is absolutely no evidence of that whatsoever.

I have the feeling that what Jesus said is what he meant. It is as hard for a rich person to get into the kingdom of God as it is for a camel to squeeze its way through a needle's eye. And the answer is, of course, that it is impossible. It is ludicrous, it is ridiculous, and I think the disciples understand that perfectly well because in verse twenty-six they respond in the way I do.

They were astonished, they were amazed, they were confused. They did not know what to think. And they said to one another, "Well, who in the world can be saved? I mean, you can't get a camel through a needle's eye. What are you talking about? How can we possibly find wholeness? How can we possibly find our way into the kingdom of God? How can we possibly get ourselves together? It is impossible." And Jesus responds, "You are right, it is impossible. It's impossible for human beings." On our own it is impossible. We cannot do it.

Now I have said a few times in my life and perhaps you have heard it said that "God has no hands but our hands." There is something interesting about that but, you know, every time I look in the mirror in the morning and look at my hands, I say to myself, "Oh, God is in big trouble. Is this all God's got? This is it." Friends, if we don't really think that God is somehow active in our lives, leading and guiding and helping us; if we think our hands are the only hands God has, we are in real big trouble and Jesus knows that, too. You see, with mortals, getting to God's kingdom is impossible; but for God, all things are possible. Everything is possible with God. Now Jesus is recording a very interesting tradition here about which I want to share one story. It comes from the Old Testament. You knew I would get to the Old Testament eventually, didn't you?

There is a story about Abraham and Sarah. You all know this story. They are a couple that God calls to be a great nation and a blessing to the entire world. The years pass, and they get older and older and older, the wrinkles begin to form, and the cellulite appears. And they get older and older and older. Suddenly, when they are a hundred years old, God comes to Abraham one day and says, "I'm going to come around here this time next year, and you are going to have a son." Abe has heard about enough of that. He just falls on his face and laughs. "You have got to be kidding! Ha, ha, have you looked at me recently, God? Have your eyes gone dim? I'm too old." And, just to make the point, God comes again to Sarah. Speaking to her, God says, "I'm going to come around here this time next year, and you are going to have a son." Sarah, listening at the tent flap, says, "Shall I, an old woman, have pleasure? Oh, this is just crazy." And she has a little laugh, too. Then God asks, "Why did you laugh?" "Oh, I didn't laugh," she says. "Oh, yes you did. Is anything too hard for the Lord?" Lo and behold, the very next year the prune-faced couple had a child. They named the infant "Isaac," which means "laughter" in Hebrew. What else would you call a baby if you had one when you were a hundred years old?

Is anything too hard for the Lord? Jesus wants to say that to us as clearly as he wants to say it to the disciples. The Hebrew Bible story also asks: Is anything too hard for the Lord? But we are not quite done yet because, you see, I don't believe it. Do you? Neither does Peter. "Oh Lord, we have left everything to follow you. I mean, I left my parents, my livelihood, my boat, my nets, everything to follow you. Don't we get the material possessions? When does it start coming?" "Oh, it is true," says Jesus. "It is a wonderful thing that you have done, that you have left brothers, sisters, mother, father, for my sake and the gospel. That is exactly right. Wonderful! And all of these things are going to come back. You are going to get a great new community of faith—people and houses, brothers, sisters, mothers, children, fields—but with persecutions." "If you follow me," Jesus says, "it is going to be hard stuff. I am not talking about easy stuff. If you want to be my disciple, you are going to have to open yourself up like a child." And there we are again, you see. Back to the child, dependent on God for God's gifts. I cannot do it on my own. As much as I think I can, as much as my own brain, my own skill, my own desire, and my own will are going to try to help me live this life, Jesus says to me, "you will never make it on your own. You absolutely will not. You simply must open yourself like a child because all gifts come from God."

Us becoming as children leads us to stewardship. The gifts of God are God's. The grace of God is from God. The things that I have in my life are loans from God. I am a steward and only a steward. I must respond to those gifts, but I can't do it on my own. I've got to open myself up dependently on God. Well, that is the choice for us. It was the same for Jesus' disciples as it is for us. You can load your camel, hop on it and try to get yourself through a needle's eye. Boy, that is a tight squeeze, friends. It's not going to make it. Or you can open yourself to God like a child, and the great gifts of God will shower. In response to those gifts, what else can you do but to give of your time and your talent and your energy and, yes, even your money? If you are absolutely dependent on God, then you too can see the rule of God in your life.

Let us pray:

Oh God, we offer you great good thanks for your innumerable gifts. We can hardly count them all. And now open us to respond so that we might see your kingdom alive with us and among us. In the name of Jesus the Christ, we pray. Amen.

An Analysis of John C. Holbert's "A Tight Squeeze"

John Holbert's "A Tight Squeeze" plays upon Jesus' "the eye of a needle" phrase. Holbert implies stewardship as he tackles believers' absolute dependence on God. He suggests that our dependence on God is akin to a child's dependence on its parents. As Holbert begins the sermon, he disarms those who assume that every preacher who talks about stewardship addresses some financial need or another. In fact, Holbert reminds the listeners that stewardship is much more than just talk about money.

He animates biblical stewardship by connecting the biblical story to contemporary people's lives. Holbert pulls off this difficult task by rendering the biblical dialogue into colloquial speech expressions. Fred Craddock, a teacher of preachers, urges his fellow pastors to design sermons that recreate dialogue, rather than merely report the conversation in a summary fashion. Holbert recreates dialogue consistently and effectively throughout the sermon.

In addition, Holbert superbly sets up a theological dichotomy for the modern mind. This rhetorical feature engages the listener in thought-provoking ways. Holbert contrasts the self-sufficiency of the rich ruler to the dependence of children. He reflects on the disciple's question, "Then who can be saved?" He then furnishes the answer: "For mortals it is impossible, but not for God; for God all things are possible." Holbert then brings Abraham's story into play. Fathering a child at the age of ninety-nine reveals the biblical truth of Holbert's point.

Finally, throughout the sermon, Holbert interjects key rhetorical questions. This speaking device engages listeners, keeping them caught up in the theological puzzles he creates. From beginning to end, listeners understand the Bible in new ways. Holbert also facilitates connections between important biblical texts that convey the theology of stewardship. On the whole, this sermon experience teaches the biblical principle of stewardship. This sermon also inspires people to become better stewards.

CHAPTER EIGHT

"CAST DOWN YOUR NETS!"

Alyce M. McKenzie

Alyce M. McKenzie describes the context for this particular sermon:

From 1996 to 1997, I served as interim senior pastor at Langhorne United Methodist Church, a church of about 600 members in Langhorne, Pennsylvania. In the sixties they had over 800 members, but events over the past decade had caused their membership to dwindle along with their morale. I preached this stewardship sermon using Jesus' command to "cast down your nets" as a metaphor for giving our gifts of time, talents, and finances to find joy in giving.

"Cast Down Your Nets!"

John 21:1-14

A key reason John wrote this Gospel was to encourage believing Christians that the risen Christ was with them, empowering them to share that good news with the whole world and to make disciples of all people. John is passionately convinced that Jesus came into the world to reconcile *everyone* to God.

In this last scene from his Gospel, John depicts the disciples as having returned from Jerusalem, which is where the death of Jesus occurred. Next, they move to Galilee where they had first met him, to all the old, familiar places where their memories of him still haunted the hills. The disciples have returned to their former fishing occupation, and are having no success.

John regards the church as the boat. Its members are the disciples who discover that the risen Christ is standing on the shore right in front of them, both commanding and empowering them to give all their energies to catching people, not fish.

Of course, Peter returned to his former trade. What else was there for him to do? He came back home from Jerusalem where he had three times told people he had never even met Jesus to save his own skin. Please don't be too hard on him unless, of course, you've never stepped forward in faith only to shrink back in fear. Peter had witnessed Jesus' gruesome execution. Now he was back home in Galilee in a spiritual shell shock of grief and guilt. Peter probably remained in his house for a long time, his head in his hands, his spirits sunk to the pits.

Then, one night, the moon was a bright sliver in the sky and a little of its light found its way into his room. He decided to go fishing. As most fishers know, fishing is usually best at night. He could sell what he caught the next morning. The other disciples came along too.

Sitting in the boat, letting down the nets, and catching nothing, they sat all night on the silvery water. Peter missed Jesus more than ever. The old song lyrics come to mind "I'll be seeing you in all the old, familiar places . . . " In all the old, familiar places Peter yearned to see Jesus' face, yet. The disciples appeared to be alone and said little, for there was nothing much to talk about anymore. Peter wondered if his companions were thinking what he was thinking—"We used to be such a grand, faith-filled group! We used to be fishers of men. When Jesus was with us, we could do anything; back then, the impossible became possible. Now, look at us. We have been here all night and not a single fish—a pathetic crew with no future."

As they rowed closer toward shore across the glimmering lake, silvery moonlight had just given way to the streaked sky of dawn. Stroke after stroke, a boat filled with empty nets and empty hearts, they rowed closer and closer to shore. Suddenly, there was a shape on the shore, getting closer. It was a person standing on the shore, waiting for them. He looked familiar—did they know him? The mist shrouded him—he materialized out of nowhere.

This has all the makings of a great Halloween scene—like something from a Stephen King novel or a Stephen Spielberg feature film. Yet the men in the boat were not afraid, but strangely comforted by this new presence. His voice floated out over the water—"Cast the net to the right side of the boat, and you will find some fish."

Now I'm not sure that I would have listened to this unidentified, mist-shrouded person. I hope I would have. But if I had already been fishing all night and caught nothing, I'm just not sure.

I know I wouldn't have done it if I had allowed my thoughts to be overpowered by the negative conviction that the best is behind me. I know people who believe that, and it's hard not to believe it sometimes when our bodies let us down, or we feel abandoned by those we love, or our numbers in worship falter. Still, even in those rough waters, there is that beckoning presence that we can't ignore on the shore of our future.

I know the mindset of some churches. "Oh, we used to be such a great church—back in the good old days. What ministries, what crowds we had then!" Jesus says simply, "Lower the nets, and you will be fishers of people." Would you have done it?

I wouldn't have lowered my net if I had immediately started listing all the reasons that lowering the nets was a bad idea that would never work. This negative thinking happens when we let the "can't" control the "can." I've known people who can be counted on, whenever a new idea or positive notion comes up, to find a reason why it won't work or why it can't be done or is simply out of the question! Sometimes I fall into that habit myself; but I've learned to spot it and ask someone more powerful than my most negative thoughts to blot it out. I've also known churches with the same syndrome. "Oh, we can't do that because—there are lots of reasons depending on the situation— we've never done it that way before, we don't have enough people to launch that kind of ministry, or we don't have the funds. The best is behind us. We can't do that because . . . Aw, come on, let's just row to shore with our empty nets and go home."

I wonder how close the disciples came to yielding to the temptation not to lower their nets. Thank God they didn't! That would have meant a retreat into spiritual despair, pulling into their shells like turtles, closing the door their Lord has opened to the future. For what Jesus is inviting them to do is to step forward in faith, to give away their fears and give themselves over in faith to their Lord. Jesus is showing them the only path to life—giving as the joy of living. I believe you know what I mean in many, daily ways when I say that our very souls need to give. When we give, we feel more joyful, more fully alive, more filled with faith. Have you ever visited a friend who was ill and taken her some flowers or soup and driven away feeling filled with the joy of giving? I've visited plenty of people in loss and sorrow who have said "I just never knew until now what a gift the support of the church is at times like this." Giving is the joy of living, for both givers and receivers.

Steve, wearing a green hospital gown, held his newborn daughter in his arms with a look of utter amazement on his face. Jeannette, his wife, smiled at her husband and new daughter from her hospital bed. It had been a tiring but successful delivery. They now had a family. Steve kept saying over and over again with a big grin on his face as rocked the baby, "I just never knew . . . I just had no clue . . . I just never realized." And then he'd start over again, "I just never knew . . . I just had no clue. . . I just never realized." Here we have a snapshot of a young father over-whelmed by the gift God has given him and his wife. He is touched to his core with the knowledge that, from now on, giv-ing love to this child will be the joy of his living. So the birth of a new child becomes the birth of a new father.

In baptism we, as a church, promise to find the joy of living in giving support and love to this new family: Greg, Michelle, and Sean. Giving bestows deeper meaning to our lives than mere tak-ing. You can all think of ways this has been true for you. As Christians, we give out of the love Christ has filled us with because we need to give to live. As we give to others, and that joy springs up in their souls, they too perpetuate the gracious cycle.

We give to live. I heard about one church that listed some-thing interesting in the weekly worship folder where it noted the weekly giving. The church listed not only plate and pledge monies, but also the hours spent by church members visiting the sick, and preparing for the Wednesday night children's dinner and the youngster's Bible study. The point was clear—"steward-ship," that word that is often narrowly connected with money, was synonymous with discipleship for this church. Stewardship is the giving of our total being in response to all God has done for us.

We give to live. We are wired that way. One of the crucial components of stewardship is giving back to God in Christ the financial gifts we have received. John Wesley had a very practi-cal, yet spiritual, formula for financial stewardship: "Earn all you can; save all you can; give all you can." Two hundred years later, that's still good advice.

This church is filled with big givers. We have big givers of time and service and devotion. Many of you give generously of your financial resources. There is room for growth in the financial aspect of our stewardship by each and every one of us. I include myself in this counsel. The tithe is the biblical standard and some of you do tithe. My husband Murry and I have been married 15 years. We have had some years that were lean and some that were not so lean. But we have committed ourselves to tithing. We feel that it has increased our joy in living as we have seen the great good that the church's ministry does here and around the world.

As part of my commitment to you over the next several months, God has led me to tithe the salary that you give to me toward the ministries of this church. There are several reasons behind this decision. I believe in these ministries. I believe in you. Most importantly, I believe in Christ who stands on the shore and challenges us to give and promises us a bountiful catch! But I still want to grow in my discipleship and in my financial stewardship as God continues to bless me. Someone told me that it is only once we have given our tithe that our offering begins.

I encourage you to fulfill your need to give more fully this year than you have in the past. Give in response to what God has given you. Give and grow in the joy of giving. Pastors do their congregations an injustice when they don't challenge them and themselves to give financially as an integral part of their faithful discipleship to God. To not offer that challenge is to rob all of us of the joy of giving. So I would encourage you to make a plan to work toward the tithe in stages. What joy we find in increasing our giving; the giving of ourselves and our financial resources! We may well hear ourselves repeating the refrain of the young father—"I never knew. . . I never realized . . . I had no clue."

Giving is a Gracious Cycle

Our giving to Langhorne United Methodist Church brings the joy of living to others. A resident from the special needs Woods School practically danced into our sanctuary last Sunday for the 2:00 P. M. service. She was so happy to be back in "her" church! It takes heat and light to have worship in a church on a chilly fall day. But because you have realized your need to give, joy springs up in a young woman's heart. You give her the chance to worship God in this beautiful sanctuary!

A grade school boy receives a Bible from the Sunday School Superintendent. His name is written inside it. He walks back to his seat proudly—this is *his* Bible! Your gift put a spring in that young boy's step and a Bible in his hands!

Our youth hear other youth witness to their faith at a Youth Rally and walk forward in faith to confess a love for Christ growing stronger in their hearts. Your gifts got them to the rally and helped them step ahead in faith!

A pastor in South Carolina sits at his desk staring at the rubble that used to be the education wing of his church. The church was burned by a racially motivated act of arson. He is asking God how his church will continue giving love and ministry with such hatred in the world and with most of its building in ruins. "Well, I may as well walk out and get the mail," he tells himself. He trudges out to the mailbox. There in the box is a check from the United Methodist Committee on Relief (UMCOR), supported by apportionments from local churches. Hope springs up in his heart that, in this world, there are people and churches that care. This newfound hope puts a spring in his step as he walks back to the front door, the only door to survive the fire. He walks through this door in faith. When you realize your need to give and contribute to this church's ministries, you have a part in putting the spring back into this pastor's step.

A young woman with two small children stopped by my office Tuesday. She had a desperate expression in her eye. "I have no place to stay tonight. Can you help me?" I was able to give them one night in a local hotel through the pastor's discretionary fund. It was a gift from all of you. You had a part in eliminating some of the desperation in the eyes of this young mother.

What if we launch a midweek children's program involving a meal and Bible study at Langhorne United Methodist Church? Your children attend, but the word gets out to the community, and children from families not currently attending church begin to participate. Through those children, new families learn of the love of Christ. Part of the financial support would come from registration fee, but part from the congregation's contributions to the ministry of this church. Wouldn't it be a wonderful feeling to know that we were helping children and their families meet Christ and place Jesus at the center of their lives? We could be

instrumental in helping them know that giving is the joy of living!

That's just one "what if?" That's just one dream for the future
of Langhorne United Methodist Church. What is your dream?
The disciples almost didn't put down their nets. But something
about Jesus' presence and his command made a connection click
for one of them and he shouted out "It is the Lord!"

May God give us in this boat called Langhorne United
Methodist Church the grace to recognize the Risen Lord standing on our shore. May God give us the grace to believe Jesus'
promise that giving is the joy of living. Let us lower the nets
together and, in the days ahead, find a great catch in waters that
we have not yet even begun to fish!

An Analysis of Alyce M. McKenzie's "Cast Down Your Nets!"

One of the small, but highly effective, ways that Alyce
McKenzie communicates with her audience is using the names of
people in the congregation. This usage is besides the names of the
biblical characters and other people named more generally (for
example, "a woman with two small children" and "a pastor in
South Carolina"). By colonizing her sermon with actual people's
names, McKenzie puts human faces on the theological points she
makes. Congregations are interested in real people and this practice effectively helps listeners connect with the message.
Sometime, when reading Luke's Gospel, notice how many names
Luke drops in relating Jesus' story. I also would suggest that
Romans 16 reveals the accommodating and more humane side of
Paul more than anything else he has written. Paul's familiarity
with the actual people to whom he writes is a measure of his pastoral concern for them.

In addition, McKenzie's use of dialogue in the sermon is effective for the same reasons. Life is full of conversation, and to recreate conversation in the pulpit gives the impression that the
congregation is present as the action takes place. Dialogue is

sprinkled throughout this sermon, the kind that every person in the sanctuary has each day. When the sermon communicates as real people speak and think, it goes a long way in establishing itself in the mind and heart of its listeners. McKenzie also uses rhetorical questions in effective ways. Strategically placed throughout the sermon, these questions help listeners focus on the matter at hand.

Finally, McKenzie throws down a powerful stewardship challenge to her congregation. She not only reveals her own stewardship practice, but also offers powerful and tangible ways that the church uses its offerings to help people. These illustrations give credible evidence of the church's dollars at work.

CHAPTER NINE

"PARKING ON SOMEONE ELSE'S NICKEL"

Douglas Mullins

Douglas Mullins describes the context for this particular sermon:

I preached "Parking on Someone Else's Nickel" on November 13, 1994. The 1,300 member St. Andrew's United Methodist Church in Findlay, Ohio, heard this sermon on Stewardship Sunday as part of the congregation's annual pledge drive. Like many churches, this church did not understand the difference between being generous and being good stewards. My church folks were very generous people and, given a good cause, would always invariably provide support. However, basic funding for the church's annual budget was never strong enough. I often spoke of the difference between benevolence and stewardship. Both are good qualities. They were quite benevolent; however, their quality of stewardship failed to match their benevolence. This sermon was early teaching about stewardship during my tenure with them.

"Parking on Someone Else's Nickel"

Matthew 25:14-30

The old train station in Cincinnati was the last of the great railroad terminals, built only a few years before passenger train service waned. Built in the Art Deco style, as you may know, the outstanding feature of Cincinnati's Union Station is its great half-dome rising up out of the west, and its great arch facing the east. One of the marvelous aspects of that immense arch is that you and a friend can stand at opposites ends of the arch, and talk to each other over that vast space. Never mind that the announcements of departing and arriving trains blare over loud speakers, and never mind that a thousand people scurry about. The sounds of your voices travel up and around that arch. You can actually whisper to each other across that distance.

From the outside, one can see the great arch from blocks away. There used to be a circular drive that came up in front of the station. If you were just going to be a few minutes, to buy a ticket or to meet an incoming train, you could park on that drive at one of the world's most frustrating parking meters.

Do you know why I call them the world's most frustrating parking meters? I call them the world's most frustrating parking meters because they didn't have a dial on them. These meters had no "face" with numbers of hours or minutes on them, no red needle pointing to the meter's remaining time. The meters were utterly blank. They were just there—nothing but a box with a slot for your coin with an invisible timer inside. So, if you were looking for a parking space and saw someone just pulling out, there was no way for you to know how much time was left on the meter. There was no safe way to play it but for you to put a nickel in the meter. You wouldn't dare try to park on someone else's nickel. For people who customarily drive around the block looking for a meter with time left on it, those meters were a big, disappointing frustration.

Did you ever do that? Did you ever drive around the block looking for a meter with time left on it? Findlay used to have meters, didn't it? Or maybe you've done that in another city. Or perhaps it was in the old Elder-Beerman parking lot right across the street. I'll bet you've looked for a meter with time on it. I call this common behavior, "parking on someone else's nickel."

We can apply the principle of parking on someone else's nickel to many areas of life. Suppose, for example, that you were sitting in a restaurant when the server brought the check to a man sitting at a nearby table. Suppose that man said to the server, "You've just ruined a great meal. I don't want this check. I'm sure the owner of this restaurant has plenty of money and can get by just fine without me paying this check." That would be a fairly clear case of parking on someone else's nickel.

Or perhaps you were waiting in line at the checkout counter in a grocery store and a woman in front of you had just a few items. What would happen if, when she got to the cashier, she said, "I only have a few items; it's no big deal, so I won't pay today. Just add a little bit to the bills of these people in line behind me." This too would amount to parking on someone else's nickel.

Parking on someone else's nickel happens in the church, too. In almost every church, and St. Andrew's is no exception, fully one-third of the people who claim membership in a church contribute absolutely nothing toward its support. Oh, they want the church there when it's time for their daughter to get married. They want the church there when someone in their family dies. They want the church there when they're in the hospital and a visit and a prayer would feel good. They want the church there on Christmas Eve so they can see the pretty candles. But they don't give anything to the church. They are parking on someone else's nickel.

Clearly, those people who give nothing to the church are not practicing good stewardship. On the other hand, there are people who do contribute to a church who aren't practicing good stewardship either.

This is Stewardship Sunday, so let's talk about stewardship. Let's get at the subject by looking at some rather common practices that may pass for stewardship, but aren't genuine acts of Christian stewardship.

It is not stewardship if, when you get a copy of the budget, you look over it and only give to those things of which you approve. Selective giving has nothing to do with stewardship.

It is not stewardship if you look at the bottom line of the budget, and then divide that number by the number of members of the church in order to determine your "fair share." The rule of thumb is that 20 percent of the people generally account for 80 percent of the giving. So, if that 20 percent decided to give only their fair share, the church would go broke in about 30 minutes. Giving your fair share isn't stewardship.

Some people use the "guilt" system to decide how much to give. They decide how little they can give without feeling guilty for not giving more.

The counterpart to the "guilt" system is the "pride" system. These people ask, "How much do I have to give in order to take pride in what I give?" I remember a man named Russell. Russell was the chairman of the Finance Committee of a church I once served. He was a successful businessman in town and had a lovely home. Russell prided himself on being the largest contributor to the church. I thought that was pretty amazing until he explained how he did it. On Pledge Sunday, he waited until people turned in all the pledge cards and then, as Finance Chair, he went through the pledge cards until he found the biggest pledge. Then he would pledge $10.00 more. I reminded him that the biblical model of stewardship began with 10 percent—a tithe—and asked him if he was doing his best. His giving went up dramatically over the next few years as he tried to step up from the roughly 5 percent he had been giving.

Neither the guilt system nor the pride system is stewardship.

So, if none of those things is stewardship, just exactly what is it? Stewardship is enumerating the ways in which God has blessed you, then asking yourself how you might respond. This is so important, I'm going to say it again: Stewardship is enumerating the ways in which God has blessed you, and then asking yourself how you might respond.

Begin with the fact that God allowed his only begotten and dearly beloved Son to die on the cross so you and I might have life in all its fullness. Move on to home and food, clothing and work, family and friends, and we soon find that virtually all that is good about life is a gift from God. Then we need to ask, "What would be an appropriate measure of my response to God's goodness?" That's stewardship. Anything less is a matter of parking on someone else's nickel.

When I set out to write a stewardship sermon to preach at St. Andrew's Church, I was stymied at first. You people meet your budget, and your giving is slightly above average. What can you say about stewardship to people who meet their budget and give more than the average? I studied the matter, and it finally dawned on me what I needed to say this morning. Two things.

The first thing is this—the only reason we are meeting our budget is by relying on the income from the St. Andrew's Foundation. You can see the effect of that in today's worship folder, where there is a report on our finances. It shows that our income for the year to date very nearly equals the budgeted needs for the year to date. But there's a footnote—an asterisk. The footnote reminds us that more than $55,000 of our income is from the Foundation, the earnings from monies that earlier generations left to the church. Relying on that extra money to cover more than 10 percent of our budget is parking on someone else's nickel.

It is my belief that we should earmark income from the foundation for special things—maintenance of this building perhaps, or programs beyond the budget—and that you and I should underwrite the budget. It will take an increase in our giving if we are going to accomplish that.

The second thing I would say is that, while we meet our budget, our budget isn't big enough. It is not a budget that will allow this church to grow. For example, a rule to guide growing churches is that a church needs the equivalent of one full-time program staff person for every 300 members, plus one to grow on. Let's see. We have more than 1,350 members, but we have only three full-time and one part-time program staff persons. We are clearly one full-time person short just to maintain, and short another one if we are going to grow. Our current budget won't accommodate any more staff, so the budget is clearly not big enough.

Let me close with a story. Belinda was a single parent, trying to take care of herself and raise five-year-old Ryan. She was a single parent because when her husband learned that the requisite surgery for her cancer would leave her disfigured, he left. One evening, Belinda tucked Ryan into bed and was reading a book to him. He interrupted her to ask if she had bought that book for him.

"Yes," she said.

He then inquired if she had also bought the bed in which he slept.

Again, the answer was, "Yes."

Had she bought the house they called home?

Yes, she had.

And what about that new sweater he liked so much?

"Yes," she said, she had bought that, too.

He thought about how good she had been to him, supplying all his needs, and finally he said, "Mommy, get my piggy bank. There are seven pennies in it. Take them and get something you really want for you."

As is so often the case, we have much to learn from our children. Ryan realized that everything he had was a gift from his mother. His response was to offer her his seven cents, everything he had. Our relationship to God is just like Ryan's relationship to his mother. Everything we have is a gift from God. Ryan offered his mother seven cents. It was not much, but it was all that he had.

An Analysis of Douglas Mullins' "Parking on Someone Else's Nickel"

This title, "Parking on Someone Else's Nickel," is an attention grabber—a great label for "unstewardship." Mullins profitably uses this image throughout his effective stewardship sermon. He opens the sermon in a roundabout way with a multitude of details that eventually wind their way back to a parking meter. This meter sets the stage for a negative image of people's stewardship. He attacks this negative image of stewardship with several concrete and easily imagined scenes that include a restaurant, a grocery store check-out line, and the church itself.

Mullins is a preacher who rewards people who listen carefully. At one point, he throws out the ironically logical statement—"There are people who do contribute to the church who aren't practicing good stewardship." This idea will pique the interest of those who are alert. He takes people down several false, but usually accepted, conventional ideas about stewardship. One by one, Mullins destroys the false logic underlying each. But even as he leads people through the minefield of faulty logic, Mullins communicates his sermon's intention. He tells the people forthrightly, "This is Stewardship Sunday, so let's talk about stewardship."

Eventually, he sets up how he wants to define stewardship by posing a rhetorical question: "So, if none of those things is stewardship, just exactly what is stewardship?" He then provides a biblical definition of stewardship and states it twice for emphasis. Near the conclusion of the sermon, he throws down a challenge to his congregation. He accomplishes this by reminding the church that, although they meet their budget, they are merely doing it by using earlier generation's gifts. Then Mullins again drops the phrase on them as he likens their stewardship performance to "parking on someone else's nickel." The conclusion comes from the words of a child. Implicit in this closing story are the words of Jesus. "Truly I tell you, unless you change and become like children, you will never enter the kingdom of heaven" (Matthew 18:3).

CHAPTER TEN

"LEGACY OF A LIGHTWEIGHT"

Philip A. Amerson

Philip A. Amerson describes the context for this particular sermon:

This sermon was preached on the behalf of our congregational leadership's concerns that our church "rarely, if ever, talked about money on Sunday morning, especially in a sermon." The leaders began to talk about money more frequently, and I consciously preached on stewardship at least twice a year. This was an early sermon that contributed to that change of focus. Up to this point, the congregation managed to "scrape by" financially. Shortly after we began to talk about our financial resources more openly, the congregation dramatically increased its annual budget and carried out a very successful capital campaign. In the end, we were probably still too cautious in talking about money and should have encouraged more laity to speak on the issue more frequently in worship and not just on the few Sundays in the fall designated as "Stewardship Sundays."

"Legacy of a Lightweight"

Romans 13:8-14; Matthew 18:21-35

"Money will buy a bed but not sleep; books, but not knowledge; food, but not an appetite; fine clothing, but not beauty; medicine, but not health; luxury, but not culture; entertainment but not happiness; a house, but not a home; a fine church building, but not spiritual joy."—(from an unpublished sermon by Dr. Thomas Lane Butts, Monroeville, Alabama, 1995).

Introduction

It was a spring morning in 1888. Alfred Nobel, the inventor of dynamite, awoke, dressed himself, and sat down for breakfast. As he flipped the pages of the morning paper, he was astonished to find his own obituary! Nobel spent his life amassing a fortune from the manufacture and sale of weapons. On that April morning, a premature obituary changed human history.

In fact, Alfred Nobel's brother had died. Yet reading this summary of his own life left Alfred overwhelmed. He saw himself as the world truly saw him—"the dynamite king," the great industrialist who made an immense fortune from explosives. The obituary accurately reported his business achievements, but captured none of his true intentions. Nobel had dreamed of a world where there would be no more wars. He wanted ignorance, prejudice, and poverty brought to an end. The obituary characterized him as one who had made a fortune by discovering new ways to mutilate and kill, not as a man of peace.

As he read his death notice, Nobel resolved that his last will and testament would be the expression of his dearest ideals.

These moments were the beginning of the "Nobel Peace Prize." The most prestigious honor bestowed to those who seek a more humane world is the result of a journalistic error.[1]

Through our lives we are writing a living legacy. As we rise and go about our routines, a subscript is being added—a legacy others perceive but perhaps cannot clearly see. The way we use our resources speaks perhaps of far different values when viewed by others. Day by day, each of us prepares a legacy with a subtext that reads "Being of sound mind, I hereby bequeath to the world . . ."

You may remember the play *Requiem for a Heavyweight* written by Rod Serling. Heavyweight boxer Mountain Rivera is confronted with the question of his legacy. He is deeply in debt. A physician tells him he must never fight again. Confused, Rivera is offered a way out by gamblers around him. If he would simply throw the fight, he would be given enough money to pay off his debts. Rivera, in desperation, mutters, "It doesn't matter; I'm dead already."

Too many of us act as if we are dead already. We fail to understand it is never too late to begin a lasting and positive legacy. Each human being, rich or poor, struggles with this question: "What legacy will I leave?" We all struggle with the complications of life. Will we behave as a spiritual lightweight or heavyweight? Neither our wealth nor our debts determine our ultimate worth. It is what we do with the resources with which we have been entrusted that makes the difference.

Upon a person's death perhaps you have heard the question, "How much did he leave?" The answer, as you well know, is "Everything!" It is true that "there are no pockets in a shroud." Perhaps we should have a warning label printed across our currency that reads: "This product can be dangerous to your spiritual health."

John Wesley, Methodism's founder, knew that we take no material possessions beyond the grave. He died with only a few pennies in his purse, yet his legacy to the world is enormous. He wrote, "I prefer that my own hands be the executors of what I possess." He was meticulous not to accumulate wealth but, rather, to be certain he gave all he could to the poor.

Consider, by contrast, Howard Hughes—one of the wealthiest men in human history. As his life came to an end, we find Hughes emaciated and alone in a hotel in Las Vegas. Hughes' wealth pushed U. S. science into new frontiers, put a camera on the moon, and helped communication satellites orbiting the globe. He did leave his mark. Yet think what more he might have given. His existence funneled down to a small, darkened bedroom where his gold and silver served no purpose other than to buy him total seclusion.

Broom Hilda, in the comic strip, is pictured discussing a legacy with her friend Irwin. "Irwin," she asks, "what would be the best way to make the world better?" He replies, "Start with yourself! Give up your bad habits and evil pleasures. Then when you're good, you'll stand as a shining example to others!" Broom Hilda thinks a moment and says, "OK, what's the second best way?"

Generosity is more a matter of spiritual self-understanding than it is a matter of financial planning. People give because they have some sense of their relationship with the Holy One and that frees them to know how to best use their checkbooks. Author Donald Kraybill writes: "It's the question of the dog and the tail. Does our faith wag our pocketbook or does our bank account wag our convictions? . . . the scriptural vision calls for a faith which influences pocketbooks."[2]

Alfred Nobel, after reading his own obituary, transcended his own personal self-concern. In order to leave a significant legacy, we need to first come to terms with the legacy we have already received. This is the message from the gospel lesson before us. God has already given to us and it is our response, our faith, that leads to a transvaluing of our everyday expectations.

What Is Our Inheritance?

Errol Smith, retired pastor of Baltimore's Lovely Lane United Methodist Church, tells of receiving a letter from the Register of

Wills in his county. He discovers he has been named in a will. "What an ecstatic feeling," he writes, "not only to be remembered so kindly, but generously as well." These were people of genuine means. Smith reports that he began to envision receiving a large gift. He might purchase a new car, an Alaskan cruise, or pay off his bills and have money in the bank.

After several months, a notice came that he should call the county court house. Smith called asking for an estimate of what he would receive from the estate. He was told that he had been left the grand sum of $100. Dr. Smith was amused by his response. He said, "I couldn't help thinking, 'Only $100!' I bought two new tires for the family station wagon. So much for the Alaskan cruise!" It's amazing how easy it is to push the button on the dashboard of our souls marked *greed*. What this family was giving was a thoughtful and generous act of the heart. Instead of my appreciating being remembered so kindly, I grew disappointed that they had not given me more, even though they were under no obligation to give me anything."[3]

We have in Matthew's Gospel, the eighteenth chapter, the parable of the merciful king and the unforgiving servant. It is an astonishing story, really. It comments on our human propensity to seek after what is best for ourselves and miss the great gifts we might share with others. Theologian Emil Brunner suggests that "The entire gospel is contained in this single parable." I think he is right. Listen again to the story.

Forgiven, Forgiving, Fore-giving

Jesus discusses with his disciples the question of how often one should forgive. Simon Peter, in typical fashion, raises his hand first. He knows that there is an appropriate limit to forgiveness. But Jesus shocks everyone by telling the parable of the merciful king and the unforgiving servant.

A debtor approaches the king seeking forgiveness. The amount owed the king is ten thousand talents. You may know that ten thousand talents is the equivalent of 50 million denarii.

A denarii is the amount paid for one day of labor. In order for this debt to be paid, he would have to turn over his paycheck every day for 150,000 years! The debt is enormous, almost inconceivable even for a nation's government. Jesus uses a sum that is the highest arithmetic number and the largest monetary unit employed in the ancient Near East. King Herod's total annual income amounted to only nine hundred talents and here the servant is being asked to pay the king ten thousand.

Clearly this is a hyperbole. Jesus stuns the hearers. He is setting his audience up for a great lesson. Now comes the first twist in the story. The groveling servant pleads for mercy. Jesus tells us that the king sets down his scepter and, like a loving parent, fully forgives the trembling, troubled servant. The king takes the mortgage paper—the bond letter—and stamps *"Paid in Full"* across this servant's mortgage. According to the parable, everything is forgiven. Such an enormous gift! It represents the enormity of the legacy we human beings have received when we are identified as God's children.

Now the parable takes another twist. Having received such a legacy, how will the servant treat others? Again, it is amazing. The servant, who has just been forgiven, leaves the king's court and behaves in an utterly inappropriate manner. On his way home, this recently forgiven servant runs across a fellow who owes him a miniscule debt. The debt would be the equivalent of a few days of labor. The forgiven servant forgets how to forgive. Does this remind you of anything? How about the prayer we pray each Sunday? You know the line: "Forgive us our debts as we forgive our debtors."

The most horrible blindness of all is when we are given great giftedness—when we are forgiven and then we take that forgiveness for granted. God is quite free to forgive or not to forgive. The parable demonstrates that to take such forgiveness for granted is a great blasphemy.

I recently had lunch with a friend. After several minutes of pleasant conversation, I asked him a question that was an old one for us. We had agreed to ask it of one another. "Tell me," I said, "how is it with your soul?" He paused. A tear formed on his cheek and he answered, "It has been six years now since my divorce and there is still bitterness. But something has changed. A month or so ago, I began to pray for my ex-spouse and all the others who hurt me. I still feel the wounds but now notice a difference. I find that I am more at peace and able to move on with my life in healthy ways."

This parable holds great exaggeration, but it also holds a great truth. This truth should touch not only our hearts but also our checkbooks. The parable suggests that, when we gather, we always come as a community of the forgiven, the forgiving, and the fore-giving.

We have been forgiven much—now, how will we behave? We are to also forgive others. This willingness to forgive is not an indifference to wrongs that have been committed, or permissiveness, or even the suggestion that we live with an absence of any ethical code. It is the understanding that to be forgiven means that we are now to take God seriously. Forgiveness means to act with positive regard toward others who have been forgiven by God as well. Then, as forgiven people who forgive, we come to the real meaning of stewardship. It is this: We are to be "fore-giving." We are to anticipate, to prepare the way, to believe in the work of God becoming manifest. This is why we give our gifts and our tithes—they are "fore-gifts;" that is, "gifts ahead of schedule," gifts preparing the way for the future. This means we will give beforehand, before we know the exact need or burden of the future. We give before the opportunities are clear or the crises arise. Like the farmer who plants the seed before gathering the crop—so we give before the harvest.

A Gratuity for God

This is the time of year when you are asked to plan for the church in the future. You are asked to make a faith commitment supporting the ministries we do together. There will always be cynics who say, "The church is always asking for money." This is not about asking for money; rather it is asking the question, "What legacy do you wish to leave?"

The claim that the church is always asking for money is categorically untrue. The church seldom asks for money and never demands it. I have discovered that some critics are able to see the short-term cost of everything while they miss the long-term value of everything! Almost everybody else in your life is asking for money, but not the church. Count up what goes to entertainment—the vacations, the movies, the club dues, the basketball or baseball games, the hobbies, and the skiing trips.

Does the church receive an equal amount? Does the church receive as much as the largest one of these other items? What legacy are you planning to leave anyway? Can you begin to imagine what this congregation might be like if we took our membership vows seriously? What if we gave the first tithe of our income to our faith community?

Why give to church? We do not give to build up a personal spiritual portfolio. We are not purchasing an "after life" insurance policy. We are not making a deal with God. Rather, we are responding to the magnificent gift that God has given us. There is no *quid pro quo* in this transaction. We give because we have already received. We give as a statement that, at the core of who we are, we know that we belong to God, that God's mercy extends to us, and, therefore, that we want to be generous in reaching others. Too many appear to give a "gratuity for God"— simply pocket change, like those coins you donate to the Salvation Army kettle at Christmas.

I remember hearing the story of a man who believed in reincarnation and spent all day, every day, simply sitting by the river, nothing else. When someone asked why he did nothing but sit by the river, he responded, "Well I've decided that I am sitting this life out . . . maybe I will do something in the next one!"

What type of obituary are you writing? What legacy are you leaving? Will your fore-gifts be those of a spiritual lightweight or a heavyweight? Hear once more the good news, the news that is graphically told in the parable from Matthew's Gospel. No matter the burden, no matter the emotional or spiritual debt you carry, the astonishing good news is that you are forgiven. The better news is that you can now be forgiving toward others. And the best news of all is this—you can, with your resources, fore-give. You don't need a second chance or another life; you don't have to sit this one out; you have a chance before you today to respond to God's gift in your life. This is your opportunity to leave a meaningful legacy. Amen.

An Analysis of Philip A. Amerson's "Legacy of a Lightweight"

"Legacy of a Lightweight" is a finely crafted sermon that places high expectations on listeners. Evidently, Amerson regularly preaches to a decidedly sophisticated audience. Almost anyone can follow the thread of Amerson's argument, but a congregation must listen intently to hear all the wisdom this sermon contains. Sophisticated or not, however, Amerson insures that the listen-ers stay with the sermon using a wide variety of striking images. Several of the "word pictures" come via other sermons, but many come from divergent arenas—movies, newspaper comic strips, books, and Amerson's day-to-day encounters with friends.

One of Amerson's strengths in this sermon was the way he "set up" the morning's text, the parable of the merciful king and the unforgiving servant (Matthew 18:21-35). He helps the listeners anticipate the parable's content when he tells them that the para-ble speaks to "our human propensity to seek after what is best for ourselves and miss the great gifts we might share with others." He places an exclamation point on his assessment when he appeals to a recognizable theological authority, Emil Brunner, who wrote, "The entire gospel is contained in this single parable."

Another effective rhetorical device Amerson uses is to furnish listeners with memory aids concerning the sermon. For example, the triad, "forgiven, forgiving, and fore-giving," effectively sum-marizes the message's content. In a sense, Amerson condenses the sermon's main thrust in a memorable "past, present, and future" format. Amerson links this triad—"forgiven, forgiving, and fore-giving"—to the rest of the sermon's stewardship content. He closes with a series of rhetorical questions that make people think about their own obituaries and their stewardship as well. Amerson's closing must have evoked serious self-examination for any person who has not thought much about the lasting legacy that she or he leaves as a disciple of Jesus.

CHAPTER ELEVEN

"TAKE THE PLUNGE!"

Laura Hollandsworth Jernigan

Laura Hollandsworth Jernigan describes the context for this sermon:

This sermon was first preached several years ago for a small congregation as part of a sermon series on stewardship. I rewrote this sermon recently challenging myself to refrain from using the word "stewardship." I wondered what it would be like to preach during "stewardship season" without once using the "S" word! As the stories spoke a bit differently this time around, I arrived with a brand-new sermon.

"Take the Plunge!"

I Kings 17:8-16; Mark 12:41-44

As a child, my father would tease me about my television-watching habits. It wasn't that I watched too much television. What my dad noticed was that I would perk up during the commercials and watch them intently, then wander off to play during the television show. I suppose I was a perfect target for advertising, for those short commercials got my attention. I sat rapt, soaking in the marketer's images and products.

I remember one particular television commercial. I even witnessed its comeback recently. The product is Nestea, the iced-tea drink mix. The commercial displays a man on a sunny and hot day standing next to a shimmering blue swimming pool. He is dressed in a suit with sweat pouring off his face. His back is toward the pool. The man grasps a glass of golden tea that jingles with ice cubes. Then, in slow motion, a camera tracks the man as he drinks the tea and falls backward into the pool, clothes and all. He hits the pool with a gigantic splash and lets out a contented, "Aahhh!" Television viewers then hear a background voice-over: "Take the Nestea Plunge!"

To live by faith is to take such a plunge. To live by faith, indeed by trust, is to let go of what we have, grasp God's promise, and then lean back and take the plunge. In those moments of risky, reckless abandon we discover how much God and others care for us. We also find out how much we care for others.

The two women we meet in today's Bible stories took the plunge. The Bible gives neither one of them a *bona fide* name. We only know them as widows. Each is famous, however, in her way. The widow of Zarephath lives in Sidon, north of Israel. She receives a visit from the prophet Elijah, who flees Israel's king. Evidently, Elijah told Ahab that it was Yahweh who controlled the rain, not Ahab's chosen god, Baal. Elijah promised a long drought to prove his point, and the drought came. So Yahweh sends Elijah north for protection and points him to our sermon's first widow. Yahweh promises Elijah that this widow will feed the prophet during the drought.

Because Sidon was a Baal-worshipping community, we can reasonably assume this widow's loyalty to Baal. Thus, the Lord does not choose her for any particular devotion to Yahweh. We also remember that she too suffers under Yahweh's imposed drought. As a woman in that time, as a widow without the help of a husband, we are certain her life was difficult to begin with, without a full-blown drought making matters worse. She has a son to care for and no resources to which to turn.

We meet her searching for left-behind sticks of firewood in order to make one last fire to shape her last handful of flour with the last bit of cooking oil. She is resigned to death, for this is the end. Suddenly, a stranger approaches and asks her to share what little last bits remain. "I'm sorry, but I can't help you. Go somewhere else, sir. There's folks better off than I who could give you something to eat." That's what I would have said if I had been in this woman's shoes. But the rules of extending hospitality to strangers in that time and place disallowed such a response. Elijah asks for a drink of water and, as the woman retrieves a drink, Elijah presses his luck and asks for a morsel of bread. At this she protests. "But . . . but I have enough only for one more cake, and that will be the last meal I will make for my child and me."

Elijah has the gall to tell her to make a cake for him first and then make one for her and her son. Moreover, Elijah tells her not to be afraid. How could Elijah know a mother's fear? This woman lived fear, fighting for the life of her child, and now she moved beyond fear to resign herself to dying of hunger and want. Afraid? No. Hopeless? Yes. Share her family's last ritual of eating and drinking with a total stranger? Why should she?

As she stands at the gate with her child lying on the floor next to her because he is too weak to move, this widow faces a huge decision. "This man says his 'god' has a word for me. This 'god' will not let my flour or oil be used up until the rains return. I don't know his 'god.' But what if I took the risk? What if I shared my flour and oil and gave this man something to eat? Would the promise of this 'god' come true for my child and me?"

Something clicks and she receives a word, a kindling of hope. The woman at Zarephath takes the plunge. She turns, goes, and makes a little cake, giving it to Elijah first. "And the jar of meal was not emptied, neither did the jug of oil fail, according to the word of the Lord." "Aahhhh!!!"

We meet the story of the second widow toward the end of Mark's Gospel. We know even less about this woman. She is in the only place the ritual law allows her in the temple, in one of the outer courts of the temple, in the Court of Women. Jesus and his disciples are there, too. Jesus watches as the tithing members of the worshipping community place their money in the trumpet-shaped treasury boxes. First, Jesus observes the rich putting in large contributions.

Then, Jesus sees a woman approach. He identifies her as a widow, one of the "least of these." He watches as she throws in her two copper coins that were worth about a quarter of a cent. Perhaps you and I might have missed her. Doubtless, we would have been more interested in counting up the total of the "big bucks." We might not have heard the tiny "clink, clink." But Jesus hears it. Her act is like music to his ears. Jesus draws the disciples' attention to her (Mark 12:43-44).

As a widow she needed every copper cent. At least she could have wisely kept one coin for her own needs and given the other one to the temple. But she took the plunge, throwing in everything she had. What could have possibly motivated this woman? I like to think that this woman had recently heard the 1 Kings story of the poor widow of Zarephath. How that widow, as poor and struggling as herself, risked her meager supply of oil and flour betting on the word of God. How she lived to see God's word fulfilled in an abundant, never-ceasing supply of flour and oil. "If God could do that for her, then what might God do for me?"

Something clicks. A word . . . a hope rekindled. The widow of Jerusalem puts her trust in the God of Israel. She walks up to the treasury and flings in her two last coins. As Jesus watches her take the plunge, he knows that his greatest plunge awaits him a short distance from the temple. For Jesus will, at great cost, walk toward the cross and give himself totally and completely to God and for the whole world.

You and I are sometimes surprised by visits from strangers or prophets with a word from the Lord. The word promises miracles and new life. But the promise of God comes with a burden—a demand for sacrifice, for giving all we have. Then God confronts us with a decision: We can hold on to what we have, to who we are; we can go on with what we have resigned ourselves to become and to a future that feels like a dead-end. Or perhaps there is a blessed alternative: We can let go and grasp the promise, as unspecified and uncertified as it might be, and take the plunge into a risky, self-giving future with the God of Israel. In those moments, we discover a jar of endless meal and a jug of never-failing oil for us to share.

Perhaps God is visiting you at this moment. Perhaps a stranger will knock on your door this week, or next month, or next year. Who is demanding your attention? What promise do you hear that sounds incredible and wonderful? What is God asking you to risk? What are you holding onto that you could "let go and let God?" Go ahead. Take the plunge. For God provides until the rains come again. When this occurs, we will have plenty to share.

An Analysis of Laura Hollandsworth Jernigan's "Take the Plunge!"

Laura Jernigan presents herself as a preacher who knows how to arrest people's attention. From the sermon's first sentence, she draws her listeners in as she relates an incident concerning her early television habits and her father teasing her about it. From her opening gambit, Jernigan describes a Nestea commercial that most of her congregation would certainly recognize. For the sermon's balance, she uses the phrase "take the plunge" as a repetitive theme. This phrase and the image it conjures effectively relate contemporary life to the biblical story. Jernigan fleshes out how two widows and the offering of their meager resources are positive examples of what stewardship calls forth.

In the exegetical portion of her sermon, Jernigan demonstrates how the widow of Zarephath and the poor widow described in Mark's Gospel both "take the plunge" by trusting God. Each offers her paltry resources based on faith, yet—almost miraculously—God does great things with these offerings. Jernigan again and again repeats the "taking the plunge" phrase for great rhetorical effect.

Jernigan, in addition, uses the practice of asking rhetorical questions to hold her congregation's attention and invite them into the preaching conversation. Most of the preachers whose sermons we offer in the volume are masters of this custom. However, Jernigan seems to have a knack for knowing when and how to employ this rhetorical convention. For example, when Jernigan asks, "What could have possibly motivated these women?" she plants seeds of another question in her listener's minds: "What motivates me?" Finally, Jernigan is also adept at connecting biblical characters' "plunge" with our own responses of faith in taking this same plunge. Jernigan opens her sermon with a child in front of the television. She finishes her sermon where believers begin to take Christian stewardship seriously—at the foot of the cross.

CHAPTER TWELVE

"GIVING: A SPIRITUAL LIFELINE"

Henry E. Roberts

Henry E. Roberts describes the context for this particular sermon:

I delivered this sermon as a prelude to a major capital campaign for our congregation of 2,700. The church runs an annual "Mission and Ministry" budget of 1.5 million. This campaign sought to underwrite the annual budget and double that amount in a capital campaign in order to build a new youth center and renovate the sanctuary. The ultimate result was that the campaign exceeded our highest expectations. Being a long-term pastor of an established but growing congregation, I have been privileged to work with many of the same key church leaders while, each year, intentionally involving new members in the process.

The problem this sermon addressed were people in our congregation who had not yet been convinced of the place of giving in their "consumer lifestyle." I hoped the sermon might permit the non-participants to envision the meaning and life enhancing quality of giving as a spiritual discipline. I sincerely attempted to enable every member of our congregation to see the crucial nature of "giving" as a life style choice. That choice then might become a means of grace.

"Giving: A Spiritual Lifeline"

Mark 12:38-44

In a recent survey of our congregation, 69 percent of the 435 people who responded to the questionnaire indicated a desire to hear more about spiritual disciplines. These folks wanted to know how they might grow spiritually. Well, let me share with you that one of the most important spiritual disciplines is "Stewardship"— otherwise known as giving or sharing. In the vernacular of the "Who Wants To Be A Millionaire" culture in which we live, one of the key lifelines is giving. "If an individual wants to receive, then he or she must give. If you want to find your life, you must give your life away." It is not fruitful for us to ask God to bless what we do or what we want—rather, we must do what God blesses.

We live in interesting times. Most of us were born on the right side of the tracks. Most of us are citizens of the United States, the land of the free and the home of the affluent. Certainly there are times when most of us have more month than money but, for the most part, it is not because of our need for basic necessities. Rather, our short-fall has to do with a high cable bill, a cell phone, orthodontic expenses, or a credit card bill. Even the poorest among us in America live better than the richest of the rich a century ago. Many of us have experienced unbelievable financial gifts. It is interesting to note that Merrill Lynch recently announced that the numbers of millionaires in the U.S. has risen almost 40 percent since 1997. Two and a half million people living in America today are millionaires. That's about 40,000 families for every state in the United States and every province in Canada. But while our wealth has increased in exploding proportions, we have begun to discover a down side. There is even a new illness referred to as "sudden wealth syndrome." The symptoms of "sudden wealth syndrome" include excessive guilt and identity confusion.

The very night that the Maryland lottery made Robert Bronson a multi-millionaire, his wife told him it would be the end of their marriage. Seventeen months later, they were divorced. Money cannot buy happiness or marital bliss. As a matter of fact, the prosperity that has soared has not only produced millionaires. Some social critics suggest our prosperity has also given us a double divorce rate, a tripled teenage suicide rate, a quadrupled rate of violent crime, and a quintupled prison population.

The sum total of all this prosperity is that we have more money, but also more bankruptcy. We have bigger houses, but smaller families. We have more conveniences, but less time. We have more medicine, but less health. We have steeper profits, but shallower relationships. We have multiplied our possessions, but reduced our values.

Magazines regularly flood our home's mailbox. Thus, I was not surprised when a catalogue featuring men's shoes recently arrived. It offered elevated shoes so that a person could be taller. I want to suggest that this offer fits the modern trend: a time of taller people who possess shorter character. One of our greatest problems is that we have learned to make more money but haven't learned to manage it. We have neglected the spiritual discipline of giving. Folks, this implication is hard to dodge—we are in trouble, serious trouble.

As a nation, we find ourselves inside a struggle between morality and economics. Robert Fogel, a Nobel Prize winning economist, recently released a new book titled *The Fourth Great Awakening and the Future of Egalitarianism.* Fogel's book addresses the conflict with current economic conditions brought about through technology and the moral values of a growing wealthy elite. His point is that we are in trouble at a time when we have more. Fogel thinks that we are not managing growing wealth very well.

Let me make two important suggestions. First of all, I would ask that we recognize that the biblical standard of the tithe is a faithful way to start managing our monies and our life. The biblical formula for Christian money management is a formula that will work. This formula simply teaches that we give 10 percent, save 10 percent, and spend the rest with joy and thanksgiving. Pay God, pay yourself, and then start living!

Jesus invites us to give, not just a tip or a tithe, but all we have in the management of our life's resources. Thus, Jesus' invitation is not so much a matter of money as it is a matter of Jesus' kingdom values. There is the interesting story in our scripture about a so-called "rich young ruler." He worried about receiving eternal life. Jesus invites him to sell his possessions and give to the poor, but he departs in deep sadness. In this morning's reading from Mark's Gospel, Jesus observes the people's gifts to Jerusalem's temple treasury. Jesus commends the widow's gift, which is "all she possesses." If this lesson doesn't make you nervous, then you are not listening. As a matter of fact, much of the scripture read today makes me nervous because Jesus criticizes the religious leaders who receive public acclaim and who offer "long prayers." I wear a "long robe," and some of you know that I occasionally pray longer than necessary. The one whom Jesus praises is not the one who gave a significant tip or a biblical tithe but, rather, the one who gave all she had. Jesus reminds all those present of an important truth: "All of them have contributed out of their abundance, but she out of her poverty has put in everything she possessed."

Jesus often leans towards the poor. He also offers a loving criticism of the powerful, influential, and wealthy, which should unnerve us as we read it 2,000 years later. As Jesus said, "It will be harder for a rich man to enter the kingdom of heaven, than for a camel to pass through the eye of a needle." Jesus was one who was born in a stable, introduced to the agony of a refugee as a child, raised in the economic backwater of Galilee, and, as a wandering teacher, had no house of his own. When Jesus taught about God's kingdom, he very clearly said "Blessed are you who are poor" (Luke 6:20). When John the Baptist asked if he was the Messiah, Jesus pointed to the fact that he "healed the sick and preached good news to the poor" (Luke 4:18). It is not about how much or how little one possesses. Understand this, it is about what and whom you trust. Our trust is in God from whom we come and unto whom we shall return.

Perhaps the great awakening for us will come when we finally wise up. I just hope it will not be too late when we finally wake up and see that we cannot take it with us. We cannot hold on to our possessions. When will we figure out when enough is enough, and begin to look for ways to creatively use our limited time and unlimited resources for good?

My second suggestion for you is to seek out and find causes to believe in. If and when you find one, plunge right in. Turn from craving success and pursue significance. Make a difference with your fortunate blessings. Give your time, your monies, your energies, and your prayers to make a difference before your day is over. God has entrusted resources to us which can do great things and make you proud but, if you don't claim giving as your lifeline, you may die with deep regret.

Leo Buscaglia has written a powerful book in which he identified three life tasks in the title: *Living, Loving, and Leaving a Legacy.* God put each of us on earth to live, to love, and to leave a legacy. By giving, we make love visible, we live our life to its fullest, and we leave a legacy.

Let me summarize our morning's message. Now that we have unraveled the question of how to make a living, we are confronted with the more important issue of how to make a life. God's word this morning is that the lifeline of giving is a starting point.

The moral of the story is best summed up in the words of the hymn "Give Of Your Best To The Master": "Gratefully seeking to serve Him, Give Him the best that you have."

An Analysis of "Giving: A Spiritual Lifeline" by Henry E. Roberts

Due to the caring and careful way Henry Roberts articulates this sermon, readers sense that Roberts has a good and long history with his listeners. This sermon is straight talk between a pastor and congregation. Roberts initiates his sermon by giving his congregation what they want—an occasion "to hear more about spiritual disciplines." In this case, the spiritual discipline is stewardship. He answers their questions and addresses the issue first raised in a congregational survey. In doing so, he implies that the sermon's agenda is really their agenda, not his.

Roberts joins Christian benevolence to modern notions of culture through stewardship. He employs phrases likely to catch the ear of contemporary people: "Who Wants To Be A Millionaire" culture, "sudden wealth syndrome," and "the Maryland lottery." Using such phrases helps Roberts convey that he too understands our modern mentality and the yearning for prosperity that accompanies it. Roberts turns this mentality against itself and suggests that, from faith's perspective, prosperity is overrated.

One of the sermon's finest sentences is Robert's lyrical indictment of the cult of prosperity. He articulates that, "We have money, but also more bankruptcy. We have bigger houses, but smaller families. We have more conveniences, but less time. We have more medicine, but less health. We have steeper profits, but shallower relationships. We have multiplied our possessions, but reduced our values." Exposing prosperity's shortcomings, Roberts offers the life-giving features of faithful stewardship. Roberts uses Jesus as an affirmative example of one who cares for the poor.

To finish, Roberts gives listeners two tangible ways to practice what he has offered in preaching. They are to first pay God, pay themselves, and then start living. Second, he recommends that people in his congregation find causes to believe in. In this way Roberts appeals to his congregation's collective will and proposes ways for them to do as Jesus did. Most congregations appreciate a pastor who communicates a course of action.

CHAPTER THIRTEEN

"EXTRAVAGANT GENEROSITY"

Adele Stiles Resmer

Adele Stiles Resmer describes the context for this particular sermon:

I preached this sermon at Little Zion Lutheran Church in Telford, Pennsylvania. It is a mid-sized congregation in a small town and rural setting that is increasingly becoming a bedroom community of Philadelphia. It is the congregation in which I did my internship some twenty years ago. About fifty percent of the congregation knows me from that time; the other fifty percent of the people are newer members.

"Extravagant Generosity"

Mark 14:3-9

She seemed to appear out of nowhere—at least that's what everyone would say when questioned about the event later. Some gathered around the table, ready to eat. Others were standing around—two here, three there, quietly talking through the events of the day. A few stragglers were just arriving when a woman brushed past them. Not pushy, but certainly with an aura of purpose. She calmly moved past the latecomers, ignored the questioning glances of those standing around, and went directly to Jesus.

Jesus, leaning on the table, deep in discussion with his host, Simon, the leper, didn't see or hear her coming. He was startled when she reached out and touched his shoulder.

All conversation came to a halt. Eyes moved from the woman to Jesus and back again. Later they would say they couldn't remember if the two had even exchanged any words. But something passed between them which they remembered most clearly.

It was the acceptance in his eyes, some said. It was the way he turned toward her, others thought. It was an imperceptible nod, still others declared.

And then she broke open a jar—they hadn't even remembered seeing it as she came in—and she poured fragrant perfumed ointment over Jesus' head. Easily a year's wages worth, they quickly figured as it ran over him, soaking his hair, dripping from his forehead and off the end of his nose, running down his shoulders, and creating little puddles by his feet on the floor.

While only a few spoke out immediately, unable to hold back their outrage—a little bit of ointment would surely have been enough, they would have to admit later—all shared a common, if unspoken, question: What was this woman doing? I don't know about you, but I have to ask the same question. What was this woman doing? I can't imagine doing something like this— butting into a dinner where I was not invited and certainly would not be welcomed, risking ridicule and dismissal, and offering a gift—poured out or otherwise—that cost a year's salary.

If she had been raised the way I was raised, and maybe the way you were too, she would have picked out a nice, tasteful, but modest gift, something that would have let Jesus know she was thinking of him and either sent it by messenger or left it discreetly at the door. She could have slipped away without making a scene. No one but Jesus would need to know that she even gave a gift. They certainly wouldn't be able to comment on the amount spent. No fuss, no muss, no ridicule or embarrassment, no extravagance or wastefulness. I definitely prefer the understated quality of this approach myself.

It is likely safe to say that this woman's parents had not raised her to make scenes either. Even if she were a wealthy woman, as her jar of expensive ointment suggests, surely her parents raised her to keep a customary modest profile—holding back rather than standing out, listening rather than speaking, gathering with women, not interrupting the men.

What happens to her? What drives her away from common custom and into such an extravagant, risky act? The woman herself gives us an important clue when she pours the fragrant ointment over Jesus' head.

This woman knows something the disciples gathered around Jesus don't know, don't understand even though Jesus has tried to tell them time and time again.

She knows that Jesus is the Messiah—the anointed one, the holy one of God. She anoints Jesus because she recognizes that Jesus is the anointed one. Makes perfect sense, doesn't it?

How she came to know this is anyone's guess. Maybe she was one of the women Jesus healed at some point in his ministry; maybe she was one of the dismissed who experienced his acceptance; maybe she heard Jesus speak of the kingdom of God.

You know, sometimes you see and hear things differently when you're not part of the inner circle, carrying a lot of preconceived ideas about what is happening and what it means.

The woman sees what the disciples can't see, that Jesus is the holy one of God, the Messiah. A Messiah who is, himself, extravagantly generous by anyone's terms—one who heals lepers who've been banished to the far edges of the community and then sits and eats with them; one who includes women among his friends and followers and then welcomes the generous gift of a bold woman; one who, in the end, gives himself completely, generously pouring himself out like a fragrant ointment over all who are lepers in one way or another, all who give gifts, and all who get outraged at such extravagance.

It is the extravagant self-giving of Jesus poured out over all in need, including this woman, that prompts, compels, and emboldens her own generosity and extravagance. Some of those who were there would later say that it was almost as if she couldn't help herself. And you know, they would be right.

Now I know that you have experienced something of the self-giving generosity of Jesus. Like this woman, you have in one way or another experienced the healing of Jesus, or have known his acceptance. You have heard through the Word, Jesus proclaiming the "in breaking" of the kingdom of God.

I know that the extravagant generosity of Jesus has poured over this congregation. And I know this because I know something of your generosity. You, like me, may not have been raised for extravagant acts—you might still admit that you are more comfortable with more modest responses. But extravagance has broken through here.

In just the part of your history that I know about, you have prayed for and supported those who have been in prison; you have held up, sometimes carried, those who have been ill; and have accompanied many as they approached death. At least one time that I know about, you filled the whole fellowship hall with clothing for those who had lost everything.

You have sent quilts to people who know little else of comfort, and today you are giving to children who are just now adding experiences of generosity to what they already know of trauma and pain. You have, to quote Deuteronomy, opened "your hand to the poor and the needy neighbor in your land" (15:11).

Your generosity has poured out and is pouring out like fragrant, expensive ointment over many—prompted by, emboldened by, and compelled by the generosity of Jesus.

Generosity that flows from the self-giving generosity of Jesus can't help but be extravagant, certainly compared to the dictates of common custom that encourages cautiousness in giving, the offering of modest gifts that let others know we are thinking of them which, in the end, require little, if anything, of us.

My prayer for you is that in the years ahead you will continue to experience the extravagant generosity of Jesus and, as a result, startle even yourselves by what you will be bold enough to do.

May those who look at this congregation say that it was almost as if you couldn't help it!

Amen.

An Analysis of Adele Stiles Resmer's "Extravagant Generosity"

Adele Stiles Resmer takes a straightforward story from Mark's Gospel and breathes into it a life worthy of other preacher's emulation. It is a difficult thing to preach a sermon that has a contemporary feel to it while at the same time refraining from modern illustrations. Book after book of "sermon illustrations" prove that "canned illustrations" have become a standard staple of recent sermon arrangement. It is a rare preacher who has the gift to carry a congregation back 2,000 years, while simultaneously encouraging them to act likewise in our modern world. Her allusions to the congregation's generosity make them feel a kinship to the woman around whom this sermon revolves.

Resmer, like Jernigan in "Take the Plunge," uses the rhetorical question to great homiletical advantage. She compares the woman's attitude to her own. She even suggests to the listeners that, if they had been raised as she was, they will understand what she is talking about. Several rhetorical questions achieve this goal: "What was this woman doing?" "What happens to her?" "What drives her away from common custom and into such an extravagant, risky act?" The questions create a deep sense of involved reflection on the listener's part.

Last, Resmer plants an odd word in the beginning of the sermon that later drives home her concluding appeal. First, Resmer states, "He was startled when she reached out and touched his shoulder." Then, near the conclusion, the odd word reappears when Resmer remarks: "My prayer for you is that in the years ahead you will continue to experience the extravagant generosity of Jesus and, as a result, startle even yourselves by what you will be bold enough to do." This use of the word "startle" has been planted early in the sermon only later to be cultivated in the final plea to the listener's will: "Go and do likewise." Resmer subtly encourages this congregation to do as the woman that Mark introduces does. Resmer elevates her as a prime example of faithful living.

CHAPTER FOURTEEN

"NETZER"

Margaret Moers Wenig

Margaret Moers Wenig describes the context for this particular sermon:

By the time I became Beth Am's rabbi, in September of 1984, the congregation had lost its beloved spiritual leader of 27 years, its building, and most of its members. When I applied to be Beth Am's rabbi, the Placement Director warned me against choosing to work there. "It's a dying congregation," he said.

I did not become Beth Am's rabbi to help the congregation grow. Beth Am's search committee never expressed an interest in numerical growth. In contrast, the young suburban congregations with whom I had also interviewed, seemed interested only in candidates' strategies for promoting their growth. I wasn't the marketing director these congregations wanted. Beth Am's search committee only asked questions about candidates' religious ideas.

Initially, Beth Am's growth was neither my agenda nor the member's agenda. After two years of listening to members' longing-filled memories of the congregation's glory days, however, I began to feel that exclusive focus on the congregation's past was not healthy. They had reason to be proud of their past. They had reason to mourn its loss. But pride in the congregation's past did not mean that the congregation couldn't also have a worthwhile future.

I watched some retired members continue to contribute their gifts and talents, while others acted as if the best years of their lives, the only valuable years, were over. I saw this exclusive focus on their congregation's past as parallel to their exclusive focus on their own past. It seemed to me that they would benefit from imagining that some creative, interesting, meaningful years might still lay ahead of them. In addition, they could benefit from remembering that the life of the Jewish people would continue beyond their own life spans.

As it happened, a real estate crunch in New York City forced younger Jews into Beth Am's out-of-the-way, lower middle class neighborhood. They began to trickle into the congregation. Growth happened to us as if in fulfillment of a prophecy.

I gave this sermon in May of 1986, on the Sabbath preceding *Yom Hashoah* (Holocaust Remembrance Day) anticipating our congregation's Annual Meeting two days hence. The sermon was meant to lay the groundwork for my annual report in which I detailed the hints of "new growth" in the congregation and began to articulate some dreams for the congregation's future.

The sermon's text, also the text for my upcoming annual report, comes from the *haftarah* (prophetic reading) prescribed for the last day of Passover, two days prior to the Sabbath on which this sermon was given.

I must say, that while money was necessary to support the new vision for Beth Am which had developed over time, raising money was never the pride of Beth Am's stewardship. The greatest gifts God gave to the founders of Beth Am were not the abilities to earn or raise money. The rich legacy the founders left to current Beth Am members was not reflected in bank statements. The most valuable assets Beth Am members now pass on to the congregation's next generation are not material assets. Their deep spirituality; seriousness of prayer; commitment to life-long learning; openness to new ideas and to debate; passion for social justice; close knit community and relationships which crossed lines of marital status, sexual orientation, and age; and their lack of pretension and ability to laugh at themselves—these are the gifts God gave Beth Am members to nurture and pass on. For them, being faithful stewards of God's gifts had little to do with the purse.

"Netzer"

Isaiah 10:33–11:1

The tall ones shall be felled,
The lofty ones cut down:
The thickets of the forest shall be hacked away with iron.
And the Lebanon trees shall fall in their majesty. (*TANAKH*)

Thus the prophet Isaiah describes the destruction of the Northern Kingdom by Assyria.

But a shoot shall grow out of the stump of Jesse,
A twig shall sprout from his stock. (*TANAKH*)

In four days we will observe *Yom Hashoah*. This congregation knows far too well that six million Jews died at the hands of the Nazis and that many more were displaced, orphaned, or widowed.

Tonight I want to tell you the story of one small group of Jews felled by Hitler's axe.

My story begins in Buchenwald, a concentration camp for "political prisoners"—Austrian Jews transferred from Dachau, Jews arrested in mass arrests after *Kristallnacht*, Polish Jews,

Russian Jews, Hungarian Jews, Jews whom the Nazis evacuated from other camps as the Soviet Army approached. In the eight years the camp operated it held 238,380 prisoners, of whom 56,549 died of hard labor, disease, hunger, pseudo-medical experiments, or outright murder.[1]

On April 11, American troops arrived to liberate the camp. From Buchenwald, the surviving inmates were transferred to Displaced Persons (D. P.) camps. No one would claim that conditions in the D. P. camps were great, but at least the inmates now knew that the Nazis could inflict no more blows. Because mere survival no longer preoccupied these Buchenwald survivors, they began to dream of a future. In the D. P. camps, a small group formed a *garin*—a kernel, a seed—and prepared to settle in Palestine and establish a *kibbutz*. On June 20th 1948, during a short cease-fire in the War of Independence, *Kibbutz Netzer* was founded. The survivors settled on a plot a little south of Tel Aviv, northwest of Jerusalem—a plot which had, from the beginning of the century, been a German farm.

In 1968, a neighboring *kibbutz* split and half of its members joined *Kibbutz Netzer*. The *kibbutz* expanded its name to N*etzer Sereni* after Enzo Sereni, the Italian Hagannah parachutist who had been a member of that neighboring group. The *kibbutz* flourished through farming and its industries. The founders now take pride in the birth of a third generation.[2]

Of all the stories from the Holocaust—those with sad endings and those with happy endings—why did I choose this one to tell you tonight? This story speaks to me of us, of Beth Am—where we have been and where we need to go.

When I came to Beth Am, person after person told me privately and officially of the trauma and pain the congregation had suffered.

Yes, I also heard about Beth Am's glorious years as a congregation of 200 with 100 children in a rigorous religious school. I heard about your beloved rabbi and orator in whom you took great pride. I heard about the Chanukah parties and Purim celebrations for which children and adults dressed in costume. But the glorious years were followed by decline. People moved out of the neighborhood. Retired members moved to Florida. Children grew up and left home. Elderly members died. Then your home on Thayer Street was sold out from under you.

Some members wanted to call it quits. Others were committed to Beth Am's survival. You scrounged around the neighborhood looking for someone to give you a home and almost failed until Hans found this place. Some said: "We will not worship in a church!" and left. Saturday morning services were discontinued. The congregation tightened its belt and fought merely to survive. Alas, Rabbi Margolies became ill and was forced to retire. Then followed a very unstable period. When I began in 1984, I was the third rabbi to serve this congregation in four years. When I met you, your feeling of loss was palpable. Your wounds were still fresh and deep. Mere survival was still very much a preoccupation. No one talked to me of the future. You only spoke of the recent and bygone past.

When something threatens survival, we direct all of our energy toward preserving life. But when survival no longer threatens, then it is time to direct one's attention not merely to the past and even present but to the future. As soon as the inmates of Buchenwald were secure in a D. P. camp—although they had no money or guarantees—they began to dream of a future. They did not dream of returning to Germany, or Austria, or Poland, or Hungary. They did not dream of trying to reconstruct life as it had been before the war. They did not dream of returning to the homes or even professions they occupied before the war. They imagined new life, not as it had been in the glorious pre-war days, but as it could be in a new land, under new conditions, in a new and changed time.

Imagine you are members of this *garin*—this pioneering group—and you have settled in Palestine and just formed a *kibbutz*. Look around you. You see beautiful lush green fields but nothing else. You see open space and lots of potential. Now choose a crop, or a few crops, and imagine them growing. Now choose an industry and picture the design of the factory. Now what do you want the houses to look like? What degree of private property do you want to permit? Where do you want the children to live and how shall they be educated? How shall work assignments be determined? What do you want the *kibbutz* to

135

offer you when you are ill or dying? Imagine a *kibbutz seder*—what do you want it to be like? By sheer will and luck you have survived Buchenwald. In the D. P. camp you have regained strength. You are now in *Eretz Yisrael*. You haven't much money, but you have a place to call home. You have each other. You have a future. You have dreams.

There is one piece of the story I have saved for last. What I saved was the meaning of the name of the *Kibbutz Netzer*. "*Netzer*" means a new green shoot. As its symbol, *Kibbutz Netzer* uses a picture of a huge strong tree, which has been cut down to a mere stump. But out of that stump grows a *netzer*: a new green shoot.

When someone cuts down a strong flourishing tree, the tree suffers trauma. For a period of time it struggles merely to survive; when mere survival is no longer at stake it lies seemingly dormant healing itself, allowing all of its energy to be expended on forming scar tissue over the wound. But then it uses its extensive root system to draw nourishment to send out new shoots. The grand old tree, which had been cut down, now reaches once again toward the sky.

We are that tree—a grand old tree, proud of its past glory and well-developed root system, a tree that was cut down to a fraction of its former size. For years, you struggled merely to stay alive and then to heal the wounds. Now a *netzer*, a new green shoot, has sprouted out of the stump and we have to send nourishment to it and enable it to grow and flourish and reach for the sky. Beth Am is not a dying congregation. Beth Am is not a congregation struggling merely to survive. Beth Am is a growing congregation.

It is time for all of us to start dreaming about Beth Am's future. Imagine yourselves as the founders of a new *kibbutz*, a new congregation. You are not merely curators of past treasures, you are its architects, its builders, you are its composers, you are its artists. What do you want Beth Am to be like in three or five or ten years? We need not limit our vision to what Beth Am was in its glorious past or "made do" with during its recent years of struggle. We can set our sights on the future and dare to dream dreams.

An Analysis of Margaret Moers Wenig's "Netzer"

Despite her congregation's despair over the future, Rabbi Wenig provides a lucid witness that every person and congregation has gifts to offer God's realm. Clearly, some individuals feel secure about their gifts and graces; however, every congregation includes people who have little confidence in the native ability that God gives them. In fact, some people honestly believe they can offer God nothing. Wenig, therefore, lays a "stewardship foundation" in this sermon. This foundation is a new vision of life and ministry for a congregation that has evidently lost, or at least forgotten, its God-given talents.

God sows stewardship's seeds in the soil of imagination and dreams. Rabbi Wenig begins her rabbinate at Beth Am at the low ebb of a formerly productive congregation. A confluence of circumstances now deprives her people of confidence and verve. Her "faithful remnant" only remembers its past. Little hope or vision lingers. Rabbi Wenig's homiletical task is to re-establish a sense of congregational worth. She thereby creates a sense of future hope.

Rabbi Wenig's sermon offers hope to people lacking hope. She achieves this by connecting her congregation's story to the story of other Jews caught in a similarly discouraging quandary. Sensitively, she weaves her congregation's story into the story of liberated Buchenwald Jews who begin anew in the Israeli *Kibbutz Netzer*.

Wenig's story of survival and anticipation motivates her present congregation to become stewards in their present reality. She uses a "lesser to greater" argument. Wenig suggests that, if others in more calamitous conditions endure with and for God, then we can too. Indeed, if the present congregation in Brooklyn Heights takes these first faltering steps, they can also step toward a more faithful stewardship. Members of her congregation can now develop into stewards of a new vision. They earn this new vision by imagining God's better time and world for them and others.

BIOGRAPHICAL INFORMATION ABOUT CONTRIBUTORS

Dr. Ronald J. Allen is Nettie Sweeney and Hugh Th. Miller Professor of Preaching and New Testament at Christian Theological Seminary, Indianapolis, Indiana. He is the author of a set of books widely used in seminary preaching courses. Among these are *Interpreting the Gospel: An Introduction to Preaching* and its companion volume *Patterns of Preaching: A Sermon Sampler*, an anthology of 34 different kinds of preaching. Dr. Allen has authored nearly twenty books on preaching topics.

Dr. Philip A. Amerson is the President of the Claremont School of Theology in Claremont, California. Previously, Amerson was the Senior Minister at First United Methodist Church in Bloomington, Indiana. He received his Ph.D. in the academic discipline of sociology of religion from Chandler School of Theology, Atlanta, Georgia.

Dr. Brian K. Bauknight is a clergy member of the Western Pennsylvania Annual Conference where he has been senior minister of Pittsburgh's 3,300-member Christ United Methodist Church since 1980. He has done extensive preaching on themes of financial stewardship, covenant discipleship, and spiritual gifts. He is the author of six books including two from Abingdon Press and three through Dimensions for Living.

Dr. Robert A. Hill is the current pastor at Asbury First United Methodist Church, Rochester, New York, an urban regional church that numbers 2,100 members. He is a long-time United Methodist minister and was elected delegate to the 2000 Jurisdictional Conference. He graduated from McGill University, Montreal, Canada. He is the author of five published books.

Dr. John C. Holbert is the Lois Craddock Perkins Professor of Homiletics at Perkins School of Theology at Southern Methodist University in Dallas, where he has taught for 22 years. He is the author of five published books and has served as interim pastor at First United Methodist Church, Dallas, and First United Methodist Church, Fort Worth.

Rev. René Rodgers Jensen is co-pastor with her husband Rick at First Christian Church, Omaha, Nebraska. She graduated with honors from Christian Theological Seminary in 1984 and previously served pastorates in the Kansas City area and Indianapolis. Jensen is the author of *And You Welcomed Me*, a guide for including new members, and *Contagious Conviction*. In 2001, Jensen received a clergy renewal grant from the Lilly Foundation.

Rev. Laura Jernigan is an ordained Presbyterian minister living in Atlanta, Georgia. Jernigan, as a gifted musician, applies her creativity in the areas of worship, music, Bible teaching, and preaching. She attended Union Theological Seminary in Richmond, Virginia, and served as pastor of Madison Presbyterian Church in Nashville, Tennessee. She and her husband served as mission workers in Kenya for one year with the Presbyterian Church of East Africa.

Dr. J. Ellsworth Kalas served as a parish pastor for nearly 40 years, including senior pastorates at First United Methodist Church, Green Bay; First United Methodist Church, Madison, Wisconsin; and Church of the Savior, Cleveland, Ohio. In 1988, he became the associate in evangelism with the World Methodist Council. In 1993, Kalas was named the first Senior Pastor in Residence at the new Beeson Center for Biblical Preaching and Church Leadership at Asbury Theological Seminary and later the Distinguished Preacher in Residence. In 2000 he became Professor of Preaching at Asbury Seminary. He is the author of a number of books and of the *Christian Believer*, a study of doctrine.

Dr. Alyce M. McKenzie is Assistant Professor of Homiletics at Perkins School of Theology. Ordained as an elder 1981, McKenzie is a member of the Central Pennsylvania Conference of the United Methodist Church. McKenzie received her B.A. in the History of Religions from Bryn Mawr College (1977), her Master of Divinity degree from the Divinity School of Duke University (1980), and her Ph.D. in homiletics from Princeton Theological Seminary in 1994. From 1994–1998 she served as Visiting Lecturer in Homiletics at Princeton Theological Seminary and as Consultant in Preaching and Worship to pastors of the Central and Eastern Conferences, UMC.

Dr. David Mosser is currently the pastor of First United Methodist Church in Graham, Texas. He attended Perkins School of Theology and the University of Texas at Austin, where he received his Ph. D. His disciplinary field is rhetoric. Mosser is the editor of *The Abingdon Preaching Annual*.

Rev. Douglas Mullins was born in St. Louis, Missouri, and attended the University of Cincinnati. He did graduate work at the Methodist Theological School in Ohio. Mullins' entire career has been as a pastor of local churches, beginning with his first student appointment in 1963. His pastoral assignments include some of the largest congregations in West Ohio.

Dr. Emery A. Percell has been pastor of Christ Church, Rockford, Illinois, since June of 1995, having served formerly as Senior Pastor of First United Methodist Church of Evanston, Wesley United Methodist Church of Aurora, and The United Church of Hyde Park in Chicago. A native of Colorado, he attended the Colorado College, Illiff School of Theology, and the University of Chicago. A member of the Northern Illinois Annual Conference, he has chaired the Council on Finance and Administration, served as Registrar for the Board of Ordained Ministry, and was elected as delegate to General and Jurisdictional Conferences.

Dr. Adele Stiles Resmer is an Associate Professor of Homiletics at the Lutheran Theological Seminary in Philadelphia, and the director of the Academy of Preachers. She is a pastor of the Evangelical Lutheran Church in America (ELCA).

Dr. Henry E. Roberts has been the pastor of Pensacola, Florida's historic First United Methodist Church for the past 18 years. Roberts serves on the Board of Ordained Ministry and has mentored many promising young pastors throughout the Southeastern United States.

Rabbi Margaret Moers Wenig is Rabbi Emerita of Beth Am, The People's Temple and Instructor of Liturgy and Homiletics at Hebrew Union College—Jewish Institute of Religion in New York City.

Dr. William H. Willimon is Dean of the Chapel and Professor of Christian Ministry at Duke University in Durham, North Carolina. He is the author of fifty books and is the editor of *Pulpit Resource,* used by over 8,000 pastors in the United States, Canada, and Australia.

A Selected Bibliography for Further Stewardship Reading

Bagwell, Timothy J. *Preaching for Giving: Proclaiming Financial Stewardship with Holy Boldness*. Nashville, TN: Discipleship Resources, 1993.

Basinger, Rebekah Burch, and Thomas H. Jeavons. *Growing Giver's Hearts: Treating Fundraising as Ministry*. San Francisco, California: Jossey-Bass Publishers Inc., 2000.

*Barrett, Wayne C. *The Church Finance Idea Book: Hundreds of Proven Ideas for Funding Your Ministry*. Nashville, TN: Discipleship Resources, 1989.

Barrett, Wayne C. *More Money—New Money—Big Money: Creative Strategies for Funding Today's Church*. Nashville, TN: Discipleship Resources, 1992.

Callahan, Kennon L. *Effective Church Finances: Fund-Raising and Budgeting for Church Leaders*. New York: HarperCollins Publishers, 1992.

Callahan, Kennon L. *Giving and Stewardship in an Effective Church: A Guide for Every Member*. New York: HarperCollins Publishers, 1992.

*Titles noted with an asterisk are out of print, but can be found at many libraries and divinity schools.

*Carter, Kenneth H. *The Pastor as Steward: Faithful Manager and Leader.* Nashville, TN: Discipleship Resources, 1991.

Carter, William G., ed. *Speaking of Stewardship: Model Sermons on Money and Possessions.* Louisville, Kentucky: Geneva Press, 1998.

Clements, C. Justin. *The Steward's Way: A Spirituality of Stewardship.* Kansas City, MO: Sheed & Ward, 1997.

Dick, Dan R. *Revolutionizing Christian Stewardship for the 21st Century: Lessons From Copernicus.* Nashville, TN: Discipleship Resources, 1997.

Donahue, Michael J., Dean R. Hoge, Patrick McNamara, and Charles Zech. *Money Matters: Personal Giving in American Churches.* Louisville, Kentucky: Westminster John Knox Press, 1996.

Fitch, Alger. *What the Bible Says About Money.* Joplin, Missouri: College Press Publishing Company, 1987.

Harrell, Costen J. *Stewardship and the Tithe.* Nashville, TN: Abingdon-Cokesbury Press, 1953.

*Holck, Manfred, Jr. *Creative Leadership Series: Church Finance in a Complex Economy.* Nashville, TN: Abingdon Press, 1983.

Joiner, Donald W. *Christians & Money: A Guide to Personal Finance.* Nashville, TN: Discipleship Resources, 1991.

*Kenneson, Philip D., and James L. Street. *Selling Out the Church: The Dangers of Church Marketing.* Nashville, TN: Abingdon Press, 1997.

*Knudsen, Raymond B. *Stewardship Enlistment and Commitment: A Design for Development in the Local Church.* Wilton, Connecticut: Morehouse-Barlow Co., Inc., 1985.

*Lindholm, Paul R. *A Manual on Christian Stewardship and Church Finance.* New York: World Horizons, 1957.

*Mather, Herbert. *Letters for All Seasons: A Year of Letters Designed to Increase Giving in Your Church.* Nashville, TN: Abingdon Press, 1993.

Miles, Ray. *Offering Meditations.* St. Louis, Missouri: Chalice Press, 1997.

*Morris, H.H. *Demystifying the Congregational Budget.* New York: The Alban Institute, Inc., 1988.

Needleman, Jacob. *Money and the Meaning of Life*. New York: Doubleday, 1991.

Schaller, Lyle E. *44 Ways to Expand the Financial Base of Your Congregation*. Nashville, TN: Abingdon Press, 1989.

*Shannon, Robert C. and J. Michael. *Stewardship Source Book: A Complete Stewardship Program for Your Church Procedures*. Cincinnati, Ohio: The Standard Publishing Company, 1987.

*Shedd, Charlie W. *How to Develop a Tithing Church*. Nashville, TN: Abingdon Press, 1961.

*Smith, Roy L. *Stewardship Studies: Brief Interpretations of 237 Stewardship Texts*. Nashville, TN: Abingdon Press, 1954.

Thomas, G. Ernest. *Spiritual Life Through Tithing*. Nashville, TN: Tidings, 1953.

*Thompson, T.K., ed. *Stewardship in Contemporary Theology*. New York: Associated Press, 1960.

Toler, Stan, and Elmer Towns. *Developing a Giving Church*. Kansas City, Missouri: Beacon Hill Press of Kansas City, 1999.

*Waddell, Richard. *Stewardship: A Response to the Gift of Creation*. Washington, DC: The Alban Institute, 1986.

*Walker, Joe W., ed. *Money in the Church: Into Our Third Century*. Nashville, TN: Abingdon Press, 1982.

Watley, William D. *Bring the Full Tithe: Sermons on the Grace of Giving*. Valley Forge, PA: Judson Press, 1995.

Wheeler, Sondra Ely. *Wealth as Peril and Obligation: The New Testament On Possessions*. Grand Rapids, Michigan: William B. Eerdmans Publishing Company, 1995.

Wuthnow, Robert. *The Crisis in the Churches: Spiritual Malaise, Fiscal Woe*. New York: Oxford University Press, Inc., 1997.

Notes

Chapter Three

1. "The Economics of It All," a lecture given at A Conference on Property and Possessions in Social and Religious Life, sponsored by the Lilly Foundation and the University of Chicago Divinity School, October 26, 2000.

Chapter Four

1. "Weekly Worship of the Christians," *The First Apology of Justin*, Chapter LXVII.

Chapter Six

1. "The Epistle to Diognetus," *The Ante-Nicene Fathers* (vol. 1), William B. Eerdmans Publishing Co., 1988, p. 26.
2. Lorraine Hansberry, *A Raisin in the Sun*, Random House, New York, 1959, p. 33.
3. Cristopher Lasch, The Social Thought of Jane Addams, Bobbs-Merrill Co., New York, 1965, p. 85.

Chapter Ten

1. Kenne Fant, *Alfred Nobel*, p. 207 and Nicholas Halasz in *Creative Brooding*, by Robert Raines, p. 21.
2. Kraybill, *The Upside-Down Kingdom*, p. 110.
3. Thanks to Dr. Errol Smith, "Heir to a Fantastic Inheritance," an unpublished sermon, 9 June 1996.

Chapter Fourteen

1. "Buchenwald," *Encyclopedia Judaica*, Keter Publishing House, Jerusalem, 1972, Vol. 4, p. 1446.
2. "Netzer Sereni," *Encyclopedia Judaica*, Vol. 12, p. 1131.